# Always on Sunday

*Memories of an Italian Childhood*

**Marcia A. Ru~~~~~**

# DEDICATION

To the memory of my mom and dad, Frank and
Mary Jane Pugliese

# Every Ride Counts as an Amtrak Guest Rewards® Member.

Learn more at AmtrakGuestRewards.com

**Passenger Receipt**

Reservation
Cancellation Code

---

This ticket is void if passenger receipt and ticket are detached

F

# Every Ride Counts as an Amtrak Guest Rewards® Member.

From the everyday rider to the every once in a while, Amtrak Guest Rewards members are always moving closer to free travel, upgrades and more.

Join us at AmtrakGuestRewards.com

## Visit Amtrak.com today.
Make your reservations online where lower fares may be available.

**CONDITIONS OF CARRIAGE.** All travel on Amtrak is subject to the Conditions of Carriage. The Conditions of Carriage are posted on Amtrak.com and available by calling 1-800-USA-RAIL. Travel on another service provider, purchased through Amtrak, is subject to that provider's tariffs. Unless otherwise specified on the ticket, this ticket is valid for carriage for 12 months after issue date. Refunds are subject to the applicable refund policies for the type of fare purchased. See Amtrak.com/refund. Amtrak tickets may only be sold or issued by Amtrak or Amtrak-authorized travel agents or tour operators. Tickets sold or issued by an unauthorized third party will be voided by Amtrak. Failure to board a train as booked will result in the entire reservation being cancelled with no refund. On unreserved Coach or unreserved Thruway services, seats may not be available and you may have to stand.

**AMTRAK**

I acknowledge receipt of ticket(s) and agree to

PATRICK/GEORGE below.

X **86** Name Class

RES# 957EAA 12DEC17 #

Ticket 1 of 1 01·01

**RETAIN DURING TRIP**

B

From **13Dec17/10:40AM** **RESERVED COACH SEAT**us

**PHILADELPHIA 30TH, PA To TRENTON, NJ** Time

To Space/Car

Accom

Not Valid Before/After

Endorsement/Restrictions

**AMTRAK GUEST REWARDS** — 7020162926 — MEMBER

Form of Payment

**ETICKET**
**DOCUMENT**

**HAS NO**
**VALUE**

Total Charge

Rail Fare

Fare Plans

Pricing Pts

Tkt. Ptr,

**ID REQD ON BOARD**

A978.8.532.32330
P1 16:18:09:0626

NRPT 96

**ETICKET TRAVEL DOCUMENT**

STOCK CONTROL NO.

TKT NO - DO NOT MARK OR STAMP IN THIS BLOCK

Baggage

**AMTRAK**

Riders

Name of Passenger

From

**SENIOR CITIZEN 62 YRS OR OLDER - I**
To Date

Carrier Train Time

Accom Space/Car

Form of Payment

Rail Fare Accom Charge

Fare Plans Total

**REFUND/EXCHNGE PENALTIES MAY APPLY.**
**OTHER TERMS AND CONDITIONS APPLY.**

PASSENGER RECEIPT

**AMTRAK**

# MILLE GRAZIE

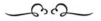

Along this journey of book writing, I quickly came to realize the immense collaboration necessary to accomplish the finished project. I thank God daily for placing the idea for this book upon my heart a few years ago and then giving me the strength, courage, and determination to make it a reality.

I couldn't have done it without the following people:

I'd like to thank Nicole DeFazio, whose enthusiasm, ideas, and editorial skills were so very much appreciated. Thank you to all who contributed — no, actually wrote — the chapter of beautiful and loving tributes to our Italian mothers. To my friends and family who helped me to form many years ago and then recapture my childhood memories — an immeasurable thank you.

Thanks to my children, Danielle, Rachel, and Anthony, whose ears I've bent and nerves I've grated, for their support and encouragement which I will forever cherish.

And last but not certainly least, thank you Sam, for being my biggest fan, agent, publicist, partner, and everything else in between. You are the best.

I'm willing to bet that you've probably received an email with the subject line: "You Know You're Italian If . . ."

If your name ends in a vowel and you can't talk without using your hands, you know without a doubt that you are Italian!

The e-mail goes something like this:

You know you're Italian if:

- Your family has spaghetti or pasta three times a week and *always on Sunday*
- You have more than one Uncle Tony
- You have an Aunt Rosa that pinches your cheek and exclaims, "Bella" every time she sees you
- You lived above or below your grandparents for some or all of your childhood
- There was a framed picture of the Pope hanging in the dining room right next to *The Last Supper*
- You had an upstairs kitchen and a downstairs kitchen
- The living room furniture was covered in clear plastic

# INTRODUCTION

I am six years old. I tightly grip my mother's white-gloved hand as we climb the steep, gray wooden steps in the back of my grandparent's house, which lead to our second floor apartment. We are returning home from Mass on a bright and sunny Sunday morning. Through the open riser of each step, I can see the cement yard below. As we ascend higher and higher, I worry that I might fall through one of the openings and land on the ground. I don't forget this frightening feeling for many years.

As afraid as I was during that climb, I love how I feel once I reach the top. Standing on that lofty space transforms me from a little girl into a princess gazing from her castle tower. The view is awesome. I see the neighboring yards, the small and tidy squares of vegetable gardens, clusters of Lily of the Valley and Rose of Sharon shrubs lining rows of fences. An old sour cherry tree covered with fluffy white blossoms dominates the small patch of grass in our tiny yard. I can see the stately steeples of St. Mary's Church only a block away—they seem close enough to reach out and touch.

My imagination soars over this panorama while I am on my perch and yet, I never stay for long. I hurry through the door and into the kitchen of the apartment where I live with my parents, Frank and Mary Jane Pugliese, and my two sisters, Sheila and Joyce. This is our home—above my paternal grandparents, Nicola and Emelia Pugliese—until I am ten years old. It is 1957.

Something changed in me when I reached middle age. I felt the distance between my present life and my past lengthen like a stretched rubber band. I felt compelled to hang on to memories of my childhood. I wanted to lasso and corral the people, places, and things that I loved. How could I slow the rampant race of time that had already stolen and faded some of my priceless memories?

I knew what I had to do. I went back to Sharpsburg, walked the streets, visited my former house and neighborhood, called old friends, asked a million questions, and finally began to remember. It was challenging at first, but like a domino effect, one memory toppled another and another and another. I began dreaming about these pockets of time and my vision became clear so that I could "see" what used to be.

I can't wipe the smile off my face when the memories flood my mind, and often I can't wipe away the tears, either.

Author Flannery O'Conner said, "Anyone who survived childhood has enough material to write for the rest of his or her life." Everyone has a story to tell. Mine is of an uncomplicated and sweet life in a small-in-size-but-large-in-love town called Sharpsburg.

# PART ONE

"...your beginnings will seem humble,
so prosperous will your future be..."

Job 8 v.7

My Nana and me, in our backyard.

# CHAPTER ONE

# ON BEING ITALIAN

Sharpsburg, Pennsylvania is located just outside of Pittsburgh. It's a typical small-town, USA dot on the map, occupied primarily by blue collar workers. There are first, second, and, now, third generation Polish and German immigrants, but the population is predominately Italian. My father used to tell my sisters and me that we were FBIs, full-blooded Italians. My husband, Sam Russotto, was born in Sicily. When we had our three children, my dad would tease us that they were only half Italian—the other half being Sicilian. By his standards, Sicily was too far removed from the mainland of Italy. My grandmother, Nana, (pronounced with a soft a) would jokingly tell us that we were related to Liberace, the famous flamboyant Italian pianist. And on St. Patrick's Day, Nana never encouraged us to wear green. Our choices were red or orange only.

Most of the Italian families living in Sharpsburg immigrated from the same small villages in Calabria, Italy. Mostly Cosenza and specifically San Pietro in Guarana. That meant we were all Calabrese. Literally, everyone knew everyone else or was somehow related. There was a well-known adage in the neighboring towns, "If you're a Panza, a Pugliese, or a Ferraro, then you're from Sharpsburg." This closeness, physical as well as familial and cultural, made Sharpsburg an ideal place to grow up, even if it meant we kids couldn't get away with anything.

Many watchful eyes of neighbors and relatives peered out of windows and doors into the backyards and the sidewalks where we played. We knew that a phone call to our parents to report unruly behavior was just a second away. Our parents knew long before Hilary Clinton did that it takes a village to raise a child! Knowing there was only a slim chance of getting away with anything curbed our escapades. Our physical, emotional and spiritual needs were met not only by our immediate family but also by our ever-present extended family of grandparents, aunts, uncles, cousins, and other relatives known as *paesans* (fellow countrymen).

My mother, Mary Jane Cerchiaro, met my father, Frank Pugliese, at a dance in Sharpsburg in 1946. People commented that they resembled Tony Curtis and Elizabeth Taylor. They married one year later and began their life by taking up residence above my paternal grandparents, Nicola Pugliese and Emelia (Tarasi). They would remain here for 15 years, until 1961.

This custom of living with one set of parents was not only encouraged in Italian families, it was expected. If you didn't live with your parents or in-laws immediately after marriage, then you lived down the street, around the corner, or a block or two away in the home of one of your *paesans*. This was how families took care of and watched out for each other.

It was a wonderful thing to live so close to my grandparents during my childhood years. It added richness and value to my childhood experience—something that is regrettably lacking in today's society. Instead of attending preschool, I spent time with my Nana in her kitchen, watching her and learning how to cook. My time with her was one priceless experience after another, and it is why I love cooking to this day.

My Tata (my grandfather) was a very quiet, pensive, and gentle soul. He was tall for an Italian, at 5' 10." I remember with such fondness the walks we took down the alley a block away to the BGI (Balda Giovanesa Italia) Club. We went late in the afternoon, just when the daily bocce games started. Tata helped build the bocce court, which is a long, narrow stretch of tamped down sand surrounded by a wooden frame. The men spent hours at that court playing bocce, smoking cigars, and sipping homemade wine until the street lights came on. That was their signal to go home. My grandfather sometimes brought me inside the club for a cold drink. Walking through the front door was like stepping into another country. It took a minute or so to adjust to the hazy smoke-filled bar. Simultaneous conversations sounded like gibberish to me, as they were in the Calabrese dialect.

Sitting on one of the worn wooden stools, sipping a ginger ale while Tata drank his beer, I felt like a celebrity. One by one, a *paesano* would approach us, make a fuss over me, and hand me a quarter or sometimes a dollar. Probably a portion of the winnings from a card game in the back room. After a while, the smoke burned my eyes and the smell of stale beer got to me and we'd head back outside.

We'd return to the bocce courts or watch a game of *More'*. This game consisted of two men simultaneously throwing out their hands with one or more fingers extended and calling out (actually shouting out!) the number they thought all of the extended fingers would equal. Basically, it was the numeric form of Rock, Paper, Scissors, and it would go on for hours. Watching *More'* is how I learned to count in Italian. I can still hear those men's voices shouting *Sette! Quattro! Otto! Nuovo!*

There were many stops on the way back home. We talked with people who were out walking or working in their garden or sitting on their porch. Tata pointed out to me how our shadows on the way home were stretched out much longer than they were on the way to the club because of the setting sun. I am so grateful for this quality time with my grandfather. I learned so much from this man who had no formal education. It didn't matter a bit. Learning something of value during a teachable moment with a grandparent adds layers of knowledge to a childhood that could never be duplicated in a classroom.

‑‑⁓‑

In the town of San Pietro in Guarano, these are the ten most common names today:

1. Intrieri
2. Bruno
3. Panza
4. Ferraro
5. Marsico
6. Bennardo
7. Imbrogno
8. Magnelli
9. Turano
10. Pugliese

An afternoon coffee break with Nana.

# CHAPTER TWO

# NANA'S CUCINA

_____ ᏻᏚ _____

Whenever I smell anise, I think of my Nana's kitchen. Anise is a sweet and pungent licorice-scented seed used in many Italian cookies and baked goods such as *pizzelles*, *biscotti*, and *frazines* (twice-baked hard and crispy rolls). My grandmother kept a small glass jar filled with these precious black anise seeds in her free-standing kitchen cupboard. They were sent to her by our relatives still living in the "old country." Nana always had a stash of black licorice candy that also came from our relatives in Calabria.

Once a month, a large package arrived at our home. It came wrapped in white muslin or sackcloth and it was tied with white cotton twine. Our address was written in indelible ink in that distinct curly-Q penmanship of someone of European descent. That anxiously awaited treasure box contained items that my grandparents just had to have. Things they missed that were not available in the U.S.

Along with the anise seeds and licorice was a tin of dried chamomile flowers, which resembled daisies. My Nana would take these sweet-smelling flowers and steep them in hot water to make a delicious dark yellow tea. This tea could cure any type of stomachache, from *agita* (indigestion) to menstrual cramps. I don't remember any of the other items

21

we received from our relatives in the old country. What I do know is that receiving those packages connected my grandparents to the loved ones they left behind in Italy.

I can still picture my grandmother, all 4'11" of her, working and cooking in her kitchen. She wore her long, gray wispy hair pulled back in a twisted knot at the nape of her neck. Standard issue for most Italian Nanas was the tiny print cotton house dress that buttoned down the front, had a narrow belt, and hit somewhere below the shin. A white half apron completed the ensemble and was not taken off until after the last dish was washed, dried, and put away at the end of the day.

Nana's kitchen was small. It was maybe 10 feet by 12 feet and sparse, yet very efficient—fitting of the décor of the 1950s. A grey Formica table, complete with red vinyl and metal chairs, sat in the center of the room and, as such, was the focal point. This table and chairs set was the only splash of color. The walls were white and the floor was grey-speckled linoleum, visibly worn in front of the sink and the stove.

My Nana's kitchen had one window, above the sink, along with one cabinet (white metal, of course). The radiator, which was next to the sink, had a duel purpose. It not only warmed the room, but also doubled as a warming drawer of sorts. Nana would rest hot pots and roasting pans on top of the radiator after they had come out of the oven or off the stove. She also used the radiator as a drying rack for the ever-present *mopine* (dish towel in the Calabrian dialect). Talk about multipurpose! This *mopine* was used for drying dishes, picking up hot pots, and covering rising bread dough. It was not uncommon to see a *mopine* on Nana's bed, covering up freshly made ravioli. Nana fashioned her own *mopines* from the sack cloth of ten-pound bags of flour. She washed the material and cut and hemmed the edges. As I said, there was no color or frills in Nana's kitchen, but she wasted nothing.

Nana's stove was standard issue—it was white with a single oven and four gas burners. Nana prepared so many wonderful meals on and in that simple appliance over the course of fifty years! Next to the stove was a free-standing white wooden cupboard with solid doors on the bottom and glass doors on the top. On the bottom were spices and other food items; the top was for dishes and cups. Nana's everyday dishes were white with white and pink dogwood flowers decorating the sides. I still have and cherish several serving pieces from that set. Nana's ice box stood in a corner of the kitchen, on a diagonal. It was quite small—only 50" high with a freezer on the upper portion that was just big enough for ice cube trays and frozen vegetables for emergencies. Nana didn't need a lot of freezer space because the majority of what came out of her kitchen was either fresh or home-made. She used the closet in the dining room as her pantry. My grandfather built shelves to house her flour, sugar, coffee, olive oil, and canned goods.

My fondest and clearest memory of Nana is watching her bake bread. When I close my eyes, I can see trickles of sweat running from her temples down past her jaw to her neck. She is standing at the kitchen table, her small strong arms and hands are working over a clump of bread dough like Rocky Balboa punishing one of his opponents in a boxing ring. A sheer mist of flour covers her arms up to her elbows. Oftentimes, she would give me a small round ball of dough to play with. I'd kneel on a kitchen chair next to her at the table and mimic her actions; kneading the smooth supple dough by pushing it away from me with the heels of my palms and pulling it back with my fingers. When Nana picked up the dough, sprinkled a handful of flour on the table to avoid sticking and then slammed the dough back down, I did the same. I loved patting the soft smooth lump, poking my fingers in it, and inhaling the yeasty, tangy odor. Baking bread was tedious. We worked the dough until it had the right amount elasticity and sheen. Then we had to let it rise for an hour before kneading it a second time. Nana and I would pour an afternoon cup of coffee, mine having more milk than coffee, while we waited on the rising dough. After that second round, it was finally time to bake. Sometimes I would watch Nana as she crocheted yet another lace doily or pillowcase for a family member.

The array of food that emerged from Nana's bread dough was amazing *and* delicious. First and foremost were the loaves of crusty bread and small sandwich buns. The smell that filled the house as they were baking was nothing short of heaven. Next were her pizzas. Every region of Italy has its own special variety of pizza that uses the ingredients plentiful in that area. The Calabrese claimed "white pizza" long before anyone had heard of it. Nana drizzled the dough with olive oil until it glistened and topped it with black cured olives, oregano, and parmesan cheese. So simple and yet absolutely perfect. The saltiness of the olives and cheese nestled in the thick and chewy olive oil-flavored dough . . . once again, heaven!

Nana's *frazines* were another Calabrian specialty. A *frazine* is an oblong-shaped roll (like a hot dog bun) speckled with anise seeds. The buns were baked and then split open and baked again until they were hard and toasted. They were perfect for dunking in coffee or hot chocolate. *Frazines* spread with butter were a favorite breakfast or late night snack. As a special treat, Nana made *pitachidas*, fried bread dough similar to doughnuts. She would fry small flat pieces of dough in oil till they were golden brown. While they were still warm, they received a dusting of sugar or salt. A plate of Nana's *pitachidas* disappeared in a New York minute.

Nana's work in her kitchen was truly a labor of love. I learned from her that every drop of sweat, every backache, and every burn mark on her arms from the furnace (her word for the oven) was well worth the enjoyment of watching her family devour and enjoy every last morsel of food placed before them. Nana's entire day centered on buying, preparing, and serving meals. Her *cucina* truly was the heart and soul of her home. I spent so many hours watching her in the kitchen, letting the traditions of our family soak in and trying to absorb all the recipes. You can't really call them recipes in the traditional sense because nothing was ever written down. Nana learned as I did, from her mother and her grandmother.

You might be wondering why my grandmother is the focus of my cooking memories instead of my mother. It's not because my mother did not cook. In Italian families, the grandmother is the matriarch who reigns over the kitchen. The role of daughters, daughters-in-law, and granddaughters is to observe and learn. That is what my mother and my sisters and I did in Nana's *cucina*. Recipes were stored in memory—not written down on paper. You had to watch in order to learn the ingredients and the techniques. I wonder if Italian women did this on purpose, so that their specialties and secrets would not leak out to other women and their families. I imagine that the women thought of themselves as the guardians of their town's recipes. There was a slight but definite streak of competitiveness when it came to deciding who made the best *pizzelles* or marinara sauce and meatballs.

It was wonderful living upstairs from my Nana and her kitchen. What a treat to be able to run downstairs and meet head on the delicious aromas that wafted through the house. And let's face it: cooking and eating to an Italian family is as important as breathing.

Me on the traveling photographer's pony

# CHAPTER THREE

# THE NEIGHBORHOOD CHARACTERS

———— ᏻ ᏻ ————

S harpsburg was a close knit, small community where mostly everyone knew everyone else. There was no need to be fearful of walking the streets, day or night. Our boundaries were delineated by blocks and street numbers. For instance, when I'd be flying out of the house to play, my mother would say to me, "Don't go past Eighth Street!" or "Stay this side of Clay Street!" or "Don't go past the church!" This gave our parents a general idea of where we would be, if we listened. This was before the days of "stranger danger" so we pretty much roamed the streets, within our limits, without fear of abductions, stalkers, and child predators.

Many self-employed vendors visited the neighborhoods of Sharpsburg on a regular basis. Our parents and grandparents did business with these people and we came to know and love them and their lively personalities. The clocks and days of the week could be set by which colorful merchant was in town.

Augie was the vegetable huckster who sold fresh produce from the back of his ancient dark green box truck. Square wicker baskets holding a variety of seasonal fruits and vegetables lined the back of his truck. He visited the produce yards, known as the Strip District, early in the morning to fill his truck with green peppers, zucchini, eggplant, tomatoes, onions, potatoes, grapes, oranges, apples, bananas— you name it, he had it. Augie's produce scale hung from the inside roof of the truck. It swung like a pendulum as he lazily crawled through the neighborhood, stopping every block or two. Women clad in their housedresses and aprons rushed out to his truck, eying up what was fresh and what was "too dear." More often than not, if someone was short a few cents Augie would wink and say, "*Va bene, basta*" (that's enough). Visiting Augie's produce truck gave the neighborhood women a chance to visit with each other and exchange the latest gossip. It was a much-needed break from the cooking and cleaning that consumed most of their day.

The scissor sharpener was Sharpsburg's most unusual visiting merchant. Can you imagine writing that occupation on a credit card application form? He didn't come around all that often and when he did, he had a lot of scissors and knives to sharpen. A traveling scissor sharpener could only make a living before everything became disposable. Back then, things were meant to last a lifetime. You took care of what you had and did not replace things as often as we do now. I still have my father's Hubbard Steel Mill letter opener etched with the saying "Hang the Load on Hubbard Hardware." We also have a punch can/bottle opener from the beer distributor on Twenty-third Street, where all of Sharpsburg bought beer and pop. Both of these items are well over fifty years old and still in use.

The ragman was a real old-timer and so was his truck. It was ancient and rusted and had a distinct rattle and creak. If you somehow managed to not hear his truck coming down the street, there was no way you could miss his singsong cry "rags and old iron!" He collected old pieces of material and broken scrap metal or machinery. No one knows what he did with his truckload of rusty junk. I think of him now as a precursor to *Sanford and Son*!

Then there was the traveling photographer whose sidekick was a pony. It was all the rage to have your child photographed sitting on a pony in the city . . . how chic! In my photo, you can see the photographer's assistant crouching behind the pony's hind legs holding me to make sure I didn't fall off. The photographer only came around during the summer and when he did, it caused quite a stir. It was a rarity to see a live pony up close, let alone right outside your house **and** leaving droppings on the sidewalk. The only other time a horse was sighted in Sharpsburg was during a Memorial Day parade. You are *really* dated if you can produce one of those photos from your family album.

My favorite merchant was the taffy apple man. His red and white truck slowly weaved its way up and down the streets. The melody he played drew the neighborhood children to him like a magnet. He wore a red and white striped shirt and a straw hat, much like a barbershop quartet member. For twenty-five cents, you could buy a tasty tart apple dipped in sweet and crunchy red taffy. And for just five cents, you could buy a pretzel rod dipped in that same thick taffy. I've yet to see a taffy covered pretzel anywhere else.

One night after dinner, I was waiting for my dad to return from buying me one of these delicious taffy apples. I was standing in the open doorway of my friend Kathy's house. Suddenly, her little brother Tommy slammed the door shut, smashing my pinky finger in the door jamb. I let out a scream that was heard a block away. Because the emergency room was across the river, my dad rushed me to the neighboring town of Etna, to Spang's Steel Mill where he worked. The nurse on duty looked at my finger, bandaged it, and sent us on our way. X-rays? Who needs X-rays? All I really cared about was getting back to eat my taffy apple. To this day my right pinky finger is crooked. I think my mother must have been at Bingo or attending the monthly Christian Mother's meeting at church when this happened.

Then there was Mrs. Serbin, the little old Jewish woman who had an entire children's clothing store in the back of her enormous Town and Country station wagon. She wore a sun visor and was so short that you could only see that visor and her small squinty eyes just barely over the steering wheel as she drove. The backseat and cargo area were packed with clothing for sale—it was like a garment district on wheels. The car was always in disarray, and Mrs. Serbin's book-keeping fit the condition of her "store." She had a huge thick book, twice the size of a phone book, with names scribbled down the side of the pages. There were slips of paper, receipts, and scraps of notes sticking out from the pages. This system apparently worked for her because she knew where every piece of clothing was and could find the exact thing you were looking for in the correct size in an instant. She sold on credit and would even let you keep an item for trial and return it the next week for a refund or exchange. She was quite the saleswoman because I remember her convincing my mother to buy clothes for us that she really couldn't afford only to return them the next time Mrs. Serbin was in the neighborhood.

Dr. Settino lived across the street from us. On almost any summer day, he could be found sitting on his massive front porch in his wicker chair, partially hidden by a curtain of cigarette smoke. From the sidewalk, you would sometimes hear a loud PSSST! This was his signal for one of us kids to climb the cement steps to the porch. The porch was darkened from the shade of the green striped canvas awning. Dr. Settino would ask his errand boy or girl to go across the street to Emma's Market to buy him a pack of Chesterfield cigarettes. It never failed that Dr. Settino's request interrupted a good game of Dodge Ball or Mother May I? No one ever minded, though, because he always tipped a dime or even a quarter, which bought a Popsicle® **and** a Bazooka bubble gum. The rule was unspoken—whoever bought Dr. Settino his cigarettes had to share the profit with everyone else. So we really didn't mind, even though we acted like we did.

No talk of the people of Sharpsburg would be complete without mentioning Pym. He lived at the end of our street on the corner of Sixth and Penn. His real name was Amedeo DeLuca, but we all called him Pym. He was married and had a son my age, Louie. Pym was like the Pied Piper of the neighborhood. Hordes of kids gathered in his yard, usually on Saturdays, and waited for Pym to lead us on a walking adventure through the streets of Sharpsburg. He was a master story teller and his tours always had several stops and a final destination. At each stop on the way, Pym would describe for us the made up character we were looking for. It was like a Peter Pan and the Lost Boys adventure. In a recent conversation, Pym's son told me that his dad's intention was to keep us kids occupied and out of trouble. He not only did that, but also kept us entertained and sparked our imagination.

Pym's excursions sometimes took us as far as Sixteenth Street, where the Sharpsburg playground was located. Mostly, though, we wound up on Ravine Street, which was the only route linking Sharpsburg to Sharpshill. In its early days, this street was dirt covered and very uneven and steep. The woods flanked either side, speckled with a few houses. This was the only place in Sharpsburg that had woods, and you know how much kids love to play in the woods! Pym would clear out an area as a makeshift campsite and it was there that we would eat our packed lunch, if we had one, and spend the afternoon enthralled in his stories. Pym was one of the few people who could tell wonderful stories without a book. Pym was a dearly loved resident of Sharpsburg. When he died in 1988, more than one thousand people attended his funeral.

The corner of Eighth and Main Street, circa. 1945

# CHAPTER FOUR

# LOAFING ON MAIN STREET

Loaf. Now *there's* a word from the past that's been lost forever, replaced by "hang out." I once asked my daughter who one of her friends was loafing with these days. You would have thought I was speaking Chinese, judging by the confused look on her face and her peels of laughter. "What are you talking about, Mom?" she asked, shaking her beautiful youthful head, puzzled.

To clear up any confusion: LOAF: (lof) verb: spend time lazily, to do very little and spend time in a lazy, wasteful way.

Quaint little towns always have a town square. You've seen it in the movies: a white Victorian gazebo on a lush green lawn surrounded by the soft glow of street lamps. A young couple holding hands strolls by under the light of a full moon. A town square was destined for loafing. Well, instead of a town square, Sharpsburg had sort of a triangle. It was here that everyone loafed, both young and old.

Main Street runs through Sharpsburg. At Tenth Street, it splits and forms a "Y," continuing to the right as Main and to the left as S. Canal Street. At that point of separation and in the middle of the triangle was a huge statue of Chief Guyasuta. He was a Seneca Indian who made his way to Sharpsburg in the late 1700s. Col. James O'Hara gave Chief Guyasuta a small parcel of land along the Allegheny River, in the vicinity of present-day Sharpsburg. General George Washington used Guyasuta as a hunter/guide during the colonial days to stake out French forts along Lake Erie. This warrior chief was instrumental and important enough in the history of Sharpsburg to honor him with his very own statue.

In our little town of Sharpsburg, there wasn't much to do **but** loaf. The boys had their spot on Main Street, in the pool hall. It was owned by someone nicknamed "Egghead," so it was referred to as either Eggheads or the pool hall. It had a strict "no girls allowed" rule. I never saw the inside of the place. My girlfriends and I loafed at Isaly's, directly across the street. I think every small town had an Isaly's. In case you don't know, Isaly's was the home of the Skyscraper ice cream cone. The ice cream was shaped into a pointed cylinder and put in a cake cone, thus the name. Isaly's was also known for their "chipped-chopped" ham, which is a thinly shaved lunch meat only available north of the Mason-Dixon Line. (Believe me, no one has ever heard of it in the South.) This ham was sometimes bathed in Isaly's own barbecue sauce and served on a soft bun, a favorite meal consumed by thousands of people in the late fifties and sixties.

Isaly's had lots of tables and chairs for its customers. When we went, we always looked for "ABC" gum stuck to the underside of these tables. If you've never heard of that type of gum, well, you're just too young. ABC stands for "already been chewed." Those hard pieces of gum had probably been on those tables for years! Gross, but definitely part of the whole Isaly's experience. After laughing about the gum, our conversation revolved around hairstyles, make-up, boys, and how our parents were just *so* unreasonable. We'd get all giggly and shy when a group of boys sauntered in after they tired of playing pool at Eggheads. The Sharpsburg

34

Isaly's was very similar to Arnold's, the hamburger place where Ritchie Cunningham, Potsie, and the Fonz loafed in the popular television series of the seventies, *Happy Days*.

On Friday nights, we'd sometimes walk over to Etna, the neighboring town, after the high school football game to go to Amato's Pizza. Once there, we'd buy a slice for ten cents and a drink for a quarter. Because there was nowhere to sit, we'd take our pizza and eat it on the walk back to Sharpsburg, which took about 20 minutes. Amato's is still in business and in the same location on Butler Street. Even today, my friends and I occasionally crave Amato's pizza and get together for "girl's nights" so we can share a pie. I've had better pizza, but eating Amato's pizza with my friends brings on a wave of nostalgia.

Sometimes we'd loaf where our friends worked. My friend Judy worked at Pontello's Bakery on the corner of Thirteenth and S. Canal Streets, giving us somewhere to go after school and on Saturdays. Sharpsburg had two bakeries: Pontello's and Rusch's. Pontello's bear claws were to die for, as were their chocolate covered strawberries, which were the size of a small child's fist and only available in the spring. We'd often go to Pontello's on Friday nights and wait for Judy to close up around seven. After that, our night of loafing could commence.

Judy's sister Donna and my friend Karen worked at a locally-owned drug store, Finelli's, which was one block away from Pontello's. It was a little more difficult for us to loaf there because Mr. Finelli usually stayed in the evenings behind the pharmacy counter, always with a close eye on whoever was working that night. The counter was elevated a step above the main floor. A locked half-door separated the pharmacy from the rest of the store. On the counter were two tall apothecary jars filled with colored water, like two soldiers on guard. We would nonchalantly stroll in, pretend we were interested in buying a jar of Noxzema or Bonne

Belle lip gloss, and whisper our plans for the night to Karen or tell her some breaking gossip (like who broke up with whom, a sighting of the boyfriend of the week, you know, really important stuff). The funniest thing I remember about Finelli's was that all the feminine products were wrapped in plain brown paper and kept on the highest shelves, only reachable with a mechanical grabber! My, weren't we modest back then? Come to think of it, one of the brand names of those feminine napkins was Modess. The magazine ad for this product read, "Modess, because . . ." Too discreet to even explain why!

Another popular place for kids of all ages was Beebe's at Main and Sixth Street. It was penny candy heaven. The sweet, strong smell of Bazooka bubble gum greeted you the second you walked in the door and onto the old wooden floor. Candy, comic books, and small toys were all for sale. Do you remember those wooden paddles with a small red rubber ball attached by a long rubber band? That paddle was Beebe's most popular item. Everyone had one and competed against each other. I never liked them because they were recycled in our house to become paddles for spanking my sisters and me when we needed it! A mere dime would get you a small brown paper bag of goodies that could possibly last the whole day, and we *did* try to stretch it. My top ten candy list includes: a red candy lipstick wrapped in gold foil, a short fat stick of chocolate licorice, a watermelon slice covered in sugar and coconut, a flying saucer wafer filled with tiny colored jimmies, (we'd save the wafer and later pretend we were receiving Holy Communion), a black licorice "record" wound around a red hard candy, a small bag of sugar babies, a white paper strip with candy buttons on it, an envelope of grape Lik'M Aid, red wax lips, and a Bazooka bubble gum, cut in half to save for later. When I was lucky enough to have an extra nickel, I would buy a Skye Bar or a Chunky. Before it burned to the ground in a fire in the early sixties, Beebe's was located on Main Street, just across from Madonna of Jerusalem Church. On days we didn't have anywhere to go, we'd buy some candy at Beebe's and go sit on the church steps, hoping that the boys would find us and loaf with us for the rest of the night.

A popular after-school stop was Emma's, one of the many small neighborhood corner stores where you could buy milk, bread, and cigarettes. Our first packs of cigarettes came from the machine in this store. A pack used to cost thirty-five cents . . . not a bad deal since we split a pack among three or four people! We really didn't smoke that much, we just wanted to be cool. A pack lasted for two weekends. One of us would store the pack in a plastic bag in our underwear drawer so the cigarettes wouldn't go stale.

Nat King Cole cleverly captured the essence of childhood summers with his song, *Lazy, Hazy, Crazy Days of Summer.* Back then, our parents did not sign us up for a number of organized sports, camps, classes at the museum, the zoo, or anything else, really. We just played outside from sun up to sun down or until the "street lights came on." Every day when it was time to head outside, we'd say to our parents, "I'm going to call on Kathy or Lois" or whomever. What that meant was that we'd go to our friend's house, stand on the sidewalk or in the back alley behind her house and literally just call her name!

We had two means of transportation around our neighborhoods. First was our bike, the second was our roller skates, the kind that went right over your shoe. It was not uncommon for a kid to keep the same pair of skates two or three years to accommodate his or her growing foot. The infamous skate key was a treasured tool that hung around our necks on a shoestring or ribbon. Sometimes I'd have my skates on all day long, only taking them off when it was lunch or dinner time.

All summer long, we kids zipped in and out and around the sidewalks, taking shortcuts through the back alleys. We had our own grid of routes to our friends' houses. We would meet in either the school or church parking lots early in the morning and plan our endless days of summer.

During the winter if it was cold enough, our parish pastor, Father Oliver, would hose down the parking lot next to the school several times a day, in the hope that a thick sheet of ice would form for skating. This was a real treat and we never minded the cold. We were city kids with no "green space" available for sled riding or other winter sports. This make-shift skating rink was as good as it got. A few times my friend Karen's dad drove a carload of us out to North Park Skating Rink. And when I say a carload, I mean fifteen or sixteen kids in one car! We sat on each other's laps in the front and back seats—this was obviously way before seatbelt laws.

From junior high through high school, we all looked forward to the once-a-month CYO dance held at Madonna Youth Center. John Tarasi, a.k.a. "Beak," spun the records for us (another phrase lost in the sixties). The girls danced together to every fast song and waited for someone to ask us to dance to a slow song. At the end of the night, the last song Beak played was always *Goodnight My Love*, by Jesse Belvin. That song was our cue to go home and dream about that certain someone with whom we were madly in love that week. Aahhh, youth really is wasted on the young!

When we were old enough to drive, we were finally able to venture out of Sharpsburg. We were eager to graduate from loafing on Main Street to loafing on Walnut Street in Shadyside, across the river. There was only one problem: no one owned a car, and I was the only one lucky enough to have a driver's license. After much begging, pleading, promising to never fight with my sisters as long as I lived, my parents agreed to let me use the family car on Wednesday nights (no such thing as two-car families back then).

My family's car was a dark green 1964 Mercury Monterey with white wall tires. The push buttons for the automatic transmission were located on the dashboard, to the right of the steering wheel. Along with the front and back windows, the rear window went up and down, at the push of a button. Pretty cool, huh? It was a four door, and almost as long as a city block. Because I drove such a colossal car, my driving skills and parallel parking skills are excellent, I must admit.

I'd pick up my girlfriends and the first thing we'd do was pool our money for gas. We only needed a quarter to get a gallon of gas and that was enough for a night of cruising. That's right, four cool girls driving the coolest boat of a car, circling from Walnut Street to Ivy Street to Kentucky Street to Aiken Street and back to Walnut, over and over and all the while acting like the most desirable girls on the planet.

If there was ever a night to be seen in Shadyside, it was Wednesday. Cars were bumper to bumper and the sidewalks were littered with kids from all over the city. A real mixture and variety of backgrounds. This was the mid-sixties. We were in the midst of the hippie era: a time of new freedom that was scary and exciting. Trends were set, trails blazed, eyes opened, mouths dropped, morals and beliefs questioned, bras burned, the draft dodged. Sit-ins, be-ins, peace rallies, love beads, bell bottoms, tie-dyed anything, peace, love, and personal freedom were all embraced. Society changed forever during that time and we, the baby boomers, had not one clue as to how instrumental we were in that pocket of history.

Sometimes when I close my eyes I imagine the summer evening's balmy breeze drifting into that car filled with laughing, hopeful teenage girls. I can smell the overpowering aroma of Ambush cologne fused with Juicy Fruit gum. The words of *Jefferson Airplane's* Gracie Slick, "Don't you want somebody to love, don't you need somebody to love?" filter out of the car's rolled down windows like fluttering confetti, mingling, then disappearing into the carnival-like atmosphere of unbridled youth and all its excitement. Far out!!

My dad, Pug (second from left), with his nicknamed
friends.

## CHAPTER FIVE

# THE NAME GAME

M y friend Judy and her sister Donna had an Uncle Ray. Every Saturday morning they woke up to their dad and Uncle Ray talking loudly at the kitchen table. All they could hear from their bedroom upstairs was, "You know who I mean, *&#!$%*!" fist pounding the table, "What was his name? Aw, Chuck, you know him! Remember he had a sister . . . they lived up there by Zucchero's? What the heck was his name? Geez, come on now, you know who I mean! You went to school with him. You know, he lived up there by Zucchero's! What was his name?!"

I guess that's what happens when you get old, we thought. When I am with my friends now and we can't recall a name from the past, we say to one another, "You know, we're *this* close to that 'Zucchero's' conversation!"

Names are more than what people call you. Names, especially nicknames, conjure up and evoke a myriad of memories. To me, it seemed like the residents of Sharpsburg were hellbent on giving everyone a nickname. I like to think these names were meant to be endearing rather than cruel, but who knows? Some nicknames were obvious, like my dad being called "Pug," short for Pugliese. Actually, there were quite a few "Pugs" as Pugliese was a common name in our town.

One of my dad's best friends was "Nanny" Panza—come to think of it, there were several of those, too. There were a couple of variations on this nickname, including "Big Nanny" and "Little Nanny." I had an Uncle "Blackie" and an Uncle "Choo." Even the mayor of Sharpsburg, Marion Gerardi, a.k.a. "Mutt," could not escape this sweeping name modification. I recently came across a yellowed article that my father saved from a 1984 edition of Sharpsburg's long-running newspaper, *The Herald*. Here is an excerpt:

> *They waited for what seemed like an eternity, unofficial "jurors" in the regular Thursday morning hearings for criminal cases in the office of Sharpsburg District Magistrate Raymond Casper.*
>
> *Suddenly, the door opened and a dapper fellow floated in under a checkered cap, rubbed his cold hands and greeted his fellow retirees. Piney had arrived.*
>
> *"Coming here gives us something to do," said Scratch. "Gives us a chance to check on who's still alive. Besides, sometimes there's an interesting case." Scratch's proper name is James Malley and he lives in O'Hara Township.*
>
> *Oh, the nicknames? "Everyone in this town has one," said 71 year old Piney, whose proper name is Frank Urso. He lives in Sharpsburg.*
>
> *There was still time before the hearings began so Scratch, 67, began scribbling a list.*
>
> *"Let's see," he began. "There's Toots (Albert Urso), and Pinocchio (Phillip Blank) and Strats (Joseph Urso) and YaYa (Joe Vita) and Pepe (Joseph DeLuca)."*
>
> *Piney, Pug (Frank Pugliese), and Rabbit (Orlando Valenza), both of Sharpsburg, were eager to help. "Don't forget Shieky (Francis Marsico) or Cousin*

*(John Malley) and Gooch (John Susi) or Bare Hands (Joe Barrone)," said Piney.*
*"What about Satchel (George Sirkowski) or Rats (Ralph Zell) and Snabs (Lou Panza)?" chimed in Pug, 67.*
*"Awe, we haven't even scratched the surface," said Rabbit, 67. "These are only a few from Sixth Street up. We didn't even start on anybody from Sixth Street down."*

All of the people mentioned in *The Herald* article were friends of my dad. My generation used nicknames too, but not as often as our elders. Maybe that was because the nuns who taught at my school put a screeching halt to that practice, making us feel guilty in that way that only nuns can.

The most well-known alias among my generation was Ritchie Artisti, a.k.a. "Football Head." His nickname needs no explanation. But Football Head's other nickname, "Three For A Quarter," does need some explaining. He earned that moniker because he was really good at making faces, funny ones at that, and he actually made a small amount of money by charging kids a quarter to see him make three funny faces. Football Head was an unusual form of entertainment for us, not to mention a pretty sly entrepreneur!

Now for some name-dropping: A pretty famous nick-named person who emerged from Sharpsburg was Clemmy "Babe" LaCava. He was the Golden Glove Boxing champ of 1949. He was named the best amateur in the country in the featherweight division, winning all nine of his fights. When he KO'd Nicky Zezza from Puerto Rico at Madison Square Garden in 1949, the referees denied him the win as the United States was in the midst of improving relations with that country. I guess they were too afraid to give the win to an American boxer over a Puerto Rican. A riot broke out in protest. To this day, everyone in Sharpsburg who heard that fight on the radio will tell you that Babe was the champ, hands down. After his short-lived career in boxing, Clemmy moved out to California and worked as a bodyguard for Burt Reynolds for twenty years. He still lives in California.

Freddie Ciaccio, another friend of my father's, was lucky enough to land a small acting part in one of the episodes of HBO's *The Sopranos*. He enjoyed the limelight for quite some time after that. Actually, if the casting director for *The Sopranos* were to ride down Main Street on any given day, he or she would find more than enough qualified characters to use as extras.

All this talk of names brings up the subject of how the politically correct euphemism "ethnic" has replaced "Italian American" and many other similar hyphenations. I am proud to call attention to my Italian background, and I don't mind being considered a hyphenated American. I think that many times first-generation immigrants may have been too quick to relinquish their loyalties to their mother country in order to make way for a new life in America, with all its golden opportunities. Many Italian immigrants changed their surnames to sound more American so they would not lose out on job opportunities. There were many derogatory names given to Italians. "Dago," "wop," "guinea," to name a few. They are all horrible sounding and carry an ugly connotation. When my parents heard these names, they would get upset but, at the same time, were amazingly tolerant. They truly learned themselves and taught us that "Sticks and stones can break my bones but names can never hurt me." With each one of these lessons, we were given the gift of truth and self-worth. I wish my parents were alive today so I could thank them again.

Another reason for nicknames is that so often, kids don't like their own name. I often wondered why my mother didn't grace me with the name "Shirley" after my idol Shirley Temple or "Patty" after Patty Duke, or my absolute favorite, Gidget? Alas, it is traditional for Italians to name their children after someone very old or deceased and not after a glamorous movie star. So, I became Marcia Amelia, my middle name after my paternal grandmother, Nana. My older sister was Sheila Rose, after our maternal grandmother, Rose. Our lucky younger sister received the most contemporary name, Joyce Lynn, after no one in particular. This made it easy to convince her as a child that she was a purchased pagan baby!

I'll explain: When we attended grade school at Madonna of Jerusalem, each class was encouraged to bring in their leftover allowances of pennies, nickels, and dimes and plunk them into a jar for overseas missions. After accumulating five dollars, which usually took months if not the entire school year, it was adoption time. We could officially adopt a "pagan baby"—a poor deprived child who lived in a hut with ten or twelve other family members and slept on a straw bed and who had no shoes. Our five dollars allowed us to spiritually adopt a child and name him or her. Naming the baby was a very big deal to our class. Of course, the name had to be approved by Sister Mary Martha, our principal. She would write our suggested names on the blackboard. No matter what we suggested, the name chosen was always Mary "something" or Joan (Joan of Arc), or Cecelia Agatha or some other martyred saint. After all, this was a child of God! If the baby was a boy, he was always named Joseph, Christopher (before he was ousted), John, or Peter. Even though we never got the name we wanted, thinking about names for our pagan baby was one of the highlights of our school year.

Another ritual involving choosing a name occurred in the sixth or seventh grade, when we were confirmed in the Catholic Church. As we became "crusaders in Christ's army," we had a chance to add a name of our choice (ha!) to our given name. But, alas, it had to be a saint's name endorsed by none other than Sister Mary Martha. So, I became Marcia Amelia Theresa, after St. Theresa, The Little Flower. My mother desperately tried to convince me to take my Aunt Lena's name because she was my sponsor for confirmation. Well, thank goodness I won because Aunt Lena's real name was Eugenia!

At last, my fifteen minutes of fame finally arrived in the late sixties. I remember so clearly that late summer day when I heard on the transistor radio that quirky little song that glamorized my name, along with a few others...Marcia, Marcia Bo Barcia Banana Bana Bo Barcia, Fee, Fie, Foe Farcia....MARCIA!!

My sister Sheila (on the left) and me (on the right), holding
our baby sister Joyce, in 1957.

# CHAPTER SIX

# WHY ITALIANS DON'T GO TO DOCTORS

—☙☙—

I've thought a lot about why so many Italian immigrants avoided the doctor's office. First and foremost, in my opinion, was the language barrier. Most new Italian immigrants spoke very little English. They must have been very intimidated by doctors. Another big issue was money. A lot of people just simply could not afford a trip to the doctor. Last, we can't forget that these new immigrants wanted and needed to hang on to the customs that connected them to the country they left behind. Even though the medical treatments I'm about to describe may sound crude, they are what the immigrants knew and trusted.

Isabel Rizzo, a *paesano* of my grandmother's, was the woman to see if you were plagued with a wart anywhere on your body and wanted it gone. I remember vividly one eerie evening in the fall of 1958, when my dad brought my sister and me to see her for just such an appointment. My wart was on my thumb; Sheila had one on her knee. According to Isabel Rizzo, the moon had to be full before the treatment could begin, which it was on that particular night as we were reluctantly ushered into her backyard. I was afraid during that mystical ceremony and refused to repeat the words Isabel recited over our warts. My sister obliged (she was older than me), and so my Dad filled in as my proxy. I remember Isabel waving herbs over the affected areas, uttering phrases in Italian, and then burying the herbs in a small, shallow grave in her yard. I had my doubts, but I knew Isabel had performed this ritual many times before, so I went along with it. And although I am not endorsing this treatment for wart removal, I do have to say that in a few days, my sister's and my warts were gone.

Sore back? Be happy you don't have to rely on this fix: A nickel was wrapped in a small piece of muslin or linen, tied with cotton string, and dipped in oil. This package was placed on the suffering person's back, on the source of the pain. The package was then lit with a match. The person conducting the treatment would immediately put a glass over the burning material. The lack of oxygen extinguished the flame and caused a vacuum to form within the glass, which in turn created suction that drew up a small mound of skin into the glass. The glass was removed, breaking the suction that had formed inside. This was repeated in several places on the back, leaving a red, round circle each time. I know many will find this procedure appalling and crude and definitely hard to visualize. I have no trouble visualizing it, as I actually watched my mother-in-law give this treatment to my husband. If you want a clearer picture of what went on, watch *The Godfather, Part Two*.

Another strange but true fix was used to treat swelling. Say you sprained your ankle—it was customary to sprinkle a piece of toast with salt and vinegar and wrap it around your ankle, where it would stay for a day or two. When it was removed, the swelling was gone. Sounds strange, but salt does draw water, right?

For colds, sniffles, and upper respiratory infections, Vicks® VapoRub® was the over-the-counter drug of choice.

This menthol-smelling ointment was rubbed, smeared, and slathered on sore throats, congested chests, and clogged nostrils. When suffering from a cold, my Uncle Charlie would take the Vick's® remedy one step further by dropping a glob into his hot coffee, letting it melt, and then down the hatch! If Vicks® didn't work, or if a cold turned into an earache that even a few warmed drips of olive oil into the ear could not fix, Dr. Settino had to be called. This was dreaded. No matter what the diagnosis, the treatment was always the same: penicillin. Whether it was a shot in the behind or 10 days of drinking white, chalky liquid, we kids hated both.

When we were stricken with the mumps, my grandfather used an indelible ink pen to draw stars on the affected puffy area. I wonder what that was all about?

*Agita*, or heartburn/upset stomach, was a no-brainer to treat. Every good Italian medicine cabinet contained a bottle of Brioschi. Just like Alka-Seltzer, the Brioschi was mixed with water and drunk quickly. I find Brioschi to be better tasting, having a more pronounced lemon flavor. If Brioshi didn't do the trick, out came the chamomile tea.

Cod liver oil was doled out by the tablespoonful to the kids in the 50s and 60s as a lubricant to keep all our "parts" moving regularly. Not pleasant to endure, but our parents *were* on to something. Today's omega three fish oil supplements claim to reduce the risk of coronary heart disease, the number one killer of us baby boomers. I suppose that everything old is new again, even in health care.

Italians are superstitious. For us, it's easy and feels natural to blame misfortune or illness on some outside force. This outside force is known as the *mal occhio*, evil eye. The *mal occhio* doesn't have anything to do with the look of an eye. It's the look that someone can give you. It is said that people with blue eyes are more likely to give you the *mal occhio*. In my opinion, this is most likely ethnic prejudice, because most Italians have brown eyes—only the invaders from the

North had blue eyes. If you are given the *mal occhio*, you are believed to be cursed . . . that curse was called the *fascinate*. This word derives from the Latin word *faschinare*, meaning to cast a spell.

So if a rash of misfortune or physical afflictions distressed a member of the community, it was believed that this person was suffering from the *fascinate*, and it was time for that person to visit one of the few Italian women of Sharpsburg who could remove this curse. Antoinette Mainolfi was one such person. She was the grandmother (Nawnaw) of my cousin, Maryann. This is what I saw take place in Nawnaw's kitchen many years ago: Maryann was seated at the kitchen table with a bowl of water in front of her. Nawnaw dripped olive oil from her finger into the bowl of water. The number of drops of olive oil that came off Nawnaw's finger revealed the severity of the *fascinate*. Nawnaw babbled a string of words and phrases, their meaning known to her alone. These words had been passed down from one generation to the next and, in short, encouraged the evil spirits to leave Maryann's body. The mood became grimmer as Nawnaw circled the room, chanting arcane phrases, not to mention burping and belching. This went on until Nawnaw felt certain that she had lifted the curse. The final step was for Nawnaw to shake salt into the water-filled bowl to see if the olive oil would separate—if it did, it was a sure sign that the ritual was a success. After Nawnaw had finished, she said to Maryann that she "had it bad."

As a trained registered nurse I, along with the general medical community, do not endorse this treatment, or most of the others. However, I would be lying if I didn't tell you that the three-day headache from which Maryann had been suffering prior to Nawnaw's ritual disappeared a few hours later.

—꒰ ꒱—

Here is the story, "Goldilocks and the Three Bears" as told by an Italian speaking broken English. This was originally passed around in the mid 1960s and it's as funny today as it was then.

### Da Tree Bearresa

Wuans apponna tiama, wuas tree berresa: mamma berra, pappa berra, e beibe berra. Liva inna contre nire foresta. Naisa ausa. Wuans da pappa, mamma e beibi go biecha. Oreday e forghette locche de dorra.

Buya enne buya commas Goldilocchesa. She gatta nattinghe to du bette maiche trobles. She puscie olla fudda dauna di maute, not leeva cromme. Den she gos appesterresa enne slipse in olla beddsa.

Laise slobbe!

Buya enne buya commesa omma da tree beressa, olla sanneborne enne senda inne shiusa. Dei gatta no fudde, dei gatta no beddesa, e watta dei gonna du to Goldiloccchesa? Tro erra oute inne streta? Colle pulissemenne?

Fetta chanza!

Goldilocchesa stei derre tree wuicasa. Eatta aute ausen omme, en guiesta bicasa dei escha erre wuans to maiche de beddsa, she sai, "Go to elle," enne ran omme craine to erre mamma, tellenerre wuat sanimabicese de tre berrese wuer.

Wuatsuse! Wuatta iu goina du? Go compleine sitty olla?

Tata carving the turkey, Thanksgiving 1954.

# CHAPTER SEVEN

# HOLIDAYS, ITALIAN STYLE

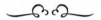

Some of my most vivid childhood memories are of the holidays. We celebrated all of our holidays "Italian style," which really meant food, food, and more food. The command *Mangia!* was heard around the clock. All you need to do to celebrate a holiday Italian style is first prepare an amazing amount of food and then throw in a lot of hearty laughter, lively conversation, painful cheek-pinching, and a genuine love for your family—it'll be *Festa Italiana* before you know it. I've worked hard to make sure that Italian customs are a large part of my family today, and I'm grateful that I love holidays as much now as I did when I was a child.

The first major holiday of the year is Easter, or *Buona Pasqua*, as we called it.

The Lenten season lasts for six weeks, ending on Easter Sunday. As Catholics, we were encouraged to give something up for Lent, such as candy, sweets or television (no one I knew ever did that). As kids, we were always looking for a creative way to deny ourselves during the Lenten season. One popular tactic was to fall in love with a vegetable right before the beginning of Lent. I remember one year I made a point to tell my mother how much I suddenly loved peas and carrots. This quickly developed into, "Gee, Mom, I think I'll give up peas and carrots for Lent this year, since I like them so much. But don't worry, you can still make them for supper, it won't bother me." Do you think she caught on? To this day, when I see peas and carrots on a dinner plate, an automatic recording plays in my head. It is my mother's voice saying, "Marcia, there are so many starving children in China. Please finish your peas and carrots!" I used to love individual pot pies, whether they were chicken, beef, or turkey. I would painstakingly remove each pea and carrot, leaving them in a small pile on my napkin. I could not understand why my mother wouldn't box them up and send them to all those poor starving children in China.

Each year during the Easter season, we'd take a trip Autenreith's, the local five and dime store on Main Street and pick out a baby chick that had been dyed a pastel color. My sisters and I each got our own. We kept the chicks in a cardboard box until their feathers grew out and became white, except for the dyed color on the tips. We then sent the chicks to their doom—a family friend's farm where they would live out their days laying eggs or becoming a roasted chicken dinner. The People for the Ethical Treatment of Animals worked to outlaw the sale of peeps many years ago.

Believe it or not, the Easter baskets filled with chocolate, jelly beans, marshmallow peeps (the edible kind), and other dentist-pleasing confections actually played second fiddle to the Easter meal. Feasting started right after Easter Sunday Mass with *frittata* and Easter bread. Our *frittata* (omelet) was made with eggs, provolone, mozzarella, ricotta, and either pepperoni or *sopressata*. Similar to pepperoni, *sopressata* is made in November or December and is left to hang in a cool, dry place until it cures. This takes about five months, making it perfect for the Easter feast. Not many people made *sopressata*, only a few old timers who prided themselves on this rare skill. If someone in your family was one of these old timers, it was a big deal. So big that our Pastor at Madonna of Jerusalem Church, Father Oliver, used his charm, cloak, and collar to get parishioners to give him *sopressata* at Easter time. Once when I was kneeling at the communion rail awaiting Holy Communion, I overheard him ask the little old Italian woman next to me in a not so low whisper, "Hey Maria, where's my *sopressata*?"

Every Holy Thursday, we made Easter bread. This egg bread is very rich and sweet and flavored with those precious anise seeds. It was served with the *frittata* in the morning and also with dinner. We had either ham or lamb, and always a form of baked pasta—ravioli, manicotti, or lasagna. The next few days we had our fill of ham sandwiches on that delicious bread. After the leftovers were gone, the diets would start . . . after all, summer was just a few months away!

Believe it or not, Memorial Day was a very big holiday for us. We anxiously awaited it and thought of it as the first holiday of the summer. Back then, Memorial Day was only one day, May 31, and not celebrated in conjunction with a weekend the way it is now. Every year, Sharpsburg held its Memorial Day parade, which was a huge event. Warm weather heralded in the debut of shorts *and* many new pairs of red, white, or blue canvas Keds, which were probably purchased at Wagner's Shoe Store.

If you were a lucky enough kid to own a bike, then you got to decorate your bike for the Memorial Day parade. It was custom to start the night before. We'd weave red, white, and blue crepe paper through the spokes of the front and back wheels. Then we'd attach tiny American flags to the backs of the seat or to the basket in the front, if you had one. We tied short streamers of crepe paper on the handle bars. Early the next morning, we proudly rode our patriotically adorned bikes to Main Street to find the perfect spot to watch the parade. We'd stand as close to the street as possible to soak in the music from the marching bands participating in the parade. I can still remember the thunderous thump, thump, thump of the throbbing drums.

Certain people always participated in the parade, including the Mayor of Sharpsburg, "Mutt" Gerardi, the Sharpsburg Volunteer Fire Department, the Ladies Auxiliary, and the Veterans of War. When the Veterans of War passed by, it was emotional as the onlookers automatically removed their caps or placed their hands over their hearts for a brief moment. The grand finale was a troupe of African American men who performed very precise dance moves set to Dixieland music. Every year they left the crowds cheering and clapping.

Even though Italians had nothing to do with Thanksgiving, we celebrated it with the rest of America. It involved eating, didn't it? Over the river and through the woods? For the first ten years of my life, Thanksgiving meant running downstairs into Nana's house, through the living/dining room, and straight into the kitchen. For big meals, my Tata turned the living room into a dining room by setting up a large wooden table and surrounding it with folding chairs. My grandfather made this table by hinging together two large pieces of wood. The legs were made of two-inch pipes that screwed into the underside of the table.

My sisters and I were responsible for setting the table while Nana, my mom, and my Aunt Mary roasted the turkey, breaded and fried cauliflower, made mashed potatoes, and perfected the sauce for the homemade ravioli they had made the day before. Until I was in my 20s I thought that everyone's Thanksgiving meal included some type of pasta bathed in tomato sauce! Dessert was always a large tray or basket filled with fresh fruit, nuts, dried figs, and dates as well as fennel, an aromatic licorice-flavored, celery-like vegetable. The token pumpkin pie was present, but we were usually too full to indulge. Besides it wasn't anyone's favorite.

A few bottles of homemade wine sat on the table. The men drank it straight up in small juice glasses and the women mixed it with Squirt or Seven-Up. The younger kids always fought over which flavor pop we would drink. We were allowed to choose a flavor from a wooden case of Regent pop. This was a special treat for us, available only on holidays. We were even allowed to drink right out of the glass bottle! Everyone wanted the cream soda flavor, and it seemed that in a case of 24 bottles, there were only three or four. In addition to minor arguments, this cream soda shortage forced us to experiment with mixing flavors. We created our own fusion drinks way ahead of our time.

After we feasted, we would sit for hours talking, laughing, teasing, and listening to stories of the "old country." I look back at those times now and see them as a primer that helped me learn to respect others, exposed me to differences of opinion, and prepared me to solve the problems that would arise in the grown-up world of my future.

Christmas was a magical time of the year for our family, like it was in so many other families. Although we were busy all season long with decorating, baking cookies, and anticipating Santa's arrival, we never forgot the true reason for Christmas: to celebrate the birth of Our Lord. Many families sang happy birthday to baby Jesus before they opened gifts.

On Christmas Eve, we celebrated the Feast of the Seven Fishes, along with most of Sharpsburg's Italian families. We still celebrate this tradition in my family today. This meal was the high point of the Christmas season. The feast includes seven types of fishes accompanied by the ever-present, predictable as an old friend, side dish of pasta. There is some debate about why there have to be seven fishes. The Catholic Church says that the number seven represents many things, including the seven sacraments, the seven days of creation, or that the number seven in biblical terms means complete. But my Nana told me that it was because seven was her favorite number. Believe what you like.

The types of fish served during the Feast of the Seven Fishes have changed over the years. When I was a child, we had to put up with the smell of dried *baccala*, which is salted cod, stiff as a board and with an odor only Pepe Le Pew could love. It was bought in advance and had to be soaked in water for days before it could be cooked. Does that tell you anything? My second least favorite was Nana's tuna and tomato sauce over pasta. Yuk! Thank goodness that's off the menu. Smelts were okay, as long as you didn't mind eating the hairy spine! The calamari was sometimes rubbery, and you don't even want to think about the eel. The mild white fish and the shrimp dishes were the most palatable. We have replaced the "old world" fish with more popular choices like salmon, orange roughy, crab cakes, linguine in clam sauce, scallop soup, and Shrimp Barsac. We still have a few family members we can't convert to seafood lovers no matter how we try. (Andrea, Samantha, Dan, you know who you are!)

After consuming that huge meal, the ham was placed in the oven and we'd leave for midnight Mass. The Mass was beautiful. First we walked into the candlelit church while the choir sung like angels. Father Oliver celebrated the entire Mass in Italian. The song *Tu Schende della Stella* (You Shine from the Stars) was a show stopper, a beautiful tribute to baby Jesus on the night of His birth. After Mass, everyone greeted each other outside with a cheery "Buon Natale!" I can't say there was always snow, but when there was it added even more to the holiday atmosphere and warm feeling. When we went back home, we were greeted by the aroma of baking ham—too much to bear! Before our coats were even off, the ham was yanked from the oven, sliced, and taste-tested by all, just to adjust the seasonings. After a nibble of ham and maybe some leftovers from dinner, we went to bed fully satiated, awaiting Christmas morning and yet another day of eating!

After the kids were asleep, friends of my parents would sometimes stop by for a little Christmas cheer or to help my father assemble toys for the coming morning madness. My sister Sheila remembers calling out to our parents after we were tucked in bed with the ruse of having to use the bathroom. No problem there! My mother came in, blindfolded Shelia, and walked her through the living room into the bathroom and back to bed again. Nothing was going to ruin our surprises from Santa.

We usually awoke pre-dawn to open presents. We were just too excited to sleep. I remember one year my younger sister Joyce asked for a Chatty Cathy Doll. But come Christmas morning, there was no such gift under the tree. She, of course, was quite distraught. My Dad called one of his friends, Sonny Galanty, the owner of Galanty's Hardware Store. He carried toys around that time of the year. If you can believe it, Sonny was kind enough to meet my Dad at the store on Christmas morning so he could buy the doll for Joyce! This was an amazing gesture on his part. But by the end of Christmas day, we were ready to gag that little blond doll because of her limited, repetitive vocabulary: "Brush my hair!" "Where are we going?" What's your name?" "I'm tired!" "I love you!"

Relatives and friends visited throughout the day while the eating frenzy continued on unabated. Large platters of homemade cookies were scattered throughout the house: in the kitchen, living room, and dining room along with dishes filled with ribbon candy, nuts, and Ferrari's Torrones (the nougat candies packed in their own little box touting the picture of an important figure in Italy's history). My mother's good friend Emily Tryc baked her famous Santa Claus cut out cookies. They were remarkable and meticulously decorated with raisins for eyes, coconut for his beard, and red colored sugar for his body. She individually wrapped each cookie, as each was a piece of art. My friend Karen and I bake a batch of these each year to give to the kids in our families. They're not as beautiful as Emily's but they are good enough to get some *oohhs* and *aahhs*.

I am proud to say that my family and I look forward to these same holiday traditions every year. They are a bridge that connects the past to the present and preserves the memories of our beloved family members who are no longer with us. Every family gathering reminds me of my parents and grandparents because of the familiar foods that are prepared and served. The aromas are another reminder of what was taught and passed on to me, solidifying my determination to preserve my family's culinary heritage, a valuable souvenir for my children and grandchildren.

My mother, Mary Jane,
ascending the steps that led to our apartment.

# CHAPTER EIGHT

# WHAT WE LEARNED FROM OUR ITALIAN MOTHERS

Soon after I began interviewing friends and relatives for this book, I saw a common thread emerge. What we cherish most is the legacy of love that we received from our families, especially our mothers. The stories I heard wove themselves into a rich and beautiful tapestry representing our collective childhood memories.

The advice and wisdom that follows came from our Italian mothers, who are forever stamped upon our hearts.

"There are so many things that I learned from my mother. Like cooking, baking, cleaning, and ironing. But all these worldly things my mother taught me are not all—she also taught me things that only a loving, caring person could.

She taught me to be strong when I felt weak, to care when it didn't seem possible, to love when all I wanted was to hate, and to believe in myself no matter what. She always said, 'If you can believe it, you can become it.'

I owe all my success in this world to my mother. It is because of her that I am strong, independent, loving, kind, and, most of all, sincere.

My mother is a true gem. There aren't many like her and I am proud to call her 'mom.'"

*Lisa DiGorio Miller, remembering her mother Philamena Cerchiaro DiGorio*

"What do you write about a mother who has always been there for you? From an early age, she displayed her unconditional love and taught me about the love Jesus had for me. She always told me that He would be there for me, and no words were ever truer.

My mother even taught me how to die. Not a moan or groan came from her mouth, just thankfulness for the blessed life Jesus had given her. Baba was and still is my hero."

*MaryAnn Pugliese Howsare, remembering her mother Raffelene Mainolfi Pugliese*

"I am the person I am today because of my mother. My mother did not believe in idle time. We cleaned, cooked, and took care of our family. Even though we worked hard, we always had a good time together. She always said to do 'good' and then forget about it. She taught me to be hard working and to do most things on my own.

She taught me to make Italian bread like my grandmother made. When my children were young and I did not work, I made it almost every week.

She made such an impression on me that I think of my mother everyday. I love her very, very much and miss her every day of my life. I often wish that I could still talk to her. She has been gone almost ten years and I have never had a dream about her. She told me once that if she could come back and talk to me, she would.

My mother was taught a ritual that supposedly removed warts. It involved the full moon, weeds, and special Italian phrases. She could not teach this to me because it had to be handed down from a female to a male. Then that male had to teach it to a female.

She was so strong and had such insight. She was always there for me and our family. Her family was her life."

*Anna Marie Rizzo Cubbage, remembering her mother Isabelle Acri Rizzo*

"There are so many things I learned from my mother, but the most important one that will always keep her alive in me is her love of cooking and feeding her family good homemade food.

I grew up the oldest of six children and remember my mom always being in the kitchen. She made many meals every day, in addition to baking Easter bread and Christmas cookies and preparing dinner for a special guest or cooking a meal for a friend who lost a loved one.

There were always kids and people in our house. My father would often comment that my mother should open a restaurant and, one day, she did. For fifteen years she served some of the best Italian food in town. Many of her regular customers who frequented *La Cresta Ristorante* in Aspinwall still talk about her delicious Fettuccini Alfredo and her signature Italian salad dressing. It was no wonder that her restaurant's motto was 'food cooked with love.'

The importance of cooking and gathering the family for Sunday dinners still exists for me and my siblings. The gesture of taking a dinner to a friend who has lost a relative is second nature, and the warmth and comfort a pot of chicken soup brings to someone suffering from the flu can never be replaced with any medicine. I learned from my mother that food not only nurtures the body but can help mend a broken spirit, set the stage for wonderful celebrations, and create memories to last a lifetime.

I may spend the rest of my life trying to make a meatball that tastes just like hers, but will never forget her hands while she was making them.

Her legacy to me has been a lifelong lesson: the beauty of food cooked with love, the laughter and happiness surrounding the kitchen table, and how entertaining is truly the spice of life."

*Karen DeFazio Flynn, remembering her mother Marianne Mazza DeFazio*

"My mom taught me right from wrong. She taught me not to lie and to always tell the truth because if she caught me in the lie, the punishment would be worse. She also taught by example—she cared and was generous to others and was active in her church.

My mom taught me how to whistle, which I thought was very cool. She taught me how to play jacks and play patty cake (which I taught to my own children). She gave me a love of books and poetry. I remember her reciting the *Midnight Ride of Paul Revere* and I can still remember the first few lines of that poem, even now.

The thing I remember most was how much she loved the soft touch of a child's hands. I love touching and holding my grandchildren because the touch of their hands brings me closer to my mom. My mother died two days before I had my second child, Christopher. I always wondered if they touched hands while they passed each other along the way."

*Mary Aiello Gauntner, remembering her mother Dolores Preston Aiello*

"I was fortunate to be raised in a family where faith in God and love were taught. From the time I was a small girl, I can remember my mother teaching me the gift of joyful giving. She was one of the most unselfish people I have ever been around. She taught me that it truly is better to give than to receive. She always said that God blesses you when you give from your heart. I saw this happen over and over again.

I was also taught that if you couldn't say anything nice about a person, don't say anything at all. My mother could always find the good in people. There were no strangers to her, only friends she hadn't met yet.

My sister and I were taught never to lie. As my mother would say, 'If I catch you in a lie, how can I ever trust you to tell the truth again?'

Another thing my mother taught me; always put garlic in meatballs and onion in meatloaf."

*Donna Litzinger Coticchia, remembering her mother Antonia Soscia Litzinger*

"Mothering skills came very easy to my mom, even though she lost her mother at the age of eight. She taught me that it is much better and rewarding to give than to receive, and to be honest, fair, and understanding.

She allowed me to express rather than to suppress my feelings. I never had to search for my soul because I already liked the one I had.

Thanks, Mom, for giving me a magical childhood, adding two loving sisters and being the center of my universe."

*Sheila Pugliese DeMare, remembering her mother Mary Jane Cerchiaro Pugliese*

"Always helping out family and friends, and having a good listening ear are some of the many things I've learned from my mother. She had so much kindness and patience. I know there were times when she didn't feel like doing something, but was there to help anyway.

One thing that made a big impression on me is that my mother never let her anger get the best of her. Believe me she did get mad at us. Using her wooden spoon to stir spaghetti sauce wasn't its only use! She would let us know she was mad and why, but ten minutes later, she'd call us for dinner as if nothing happened. Okay, sometimes I was sent to the front patio to finish my dinner when my cousin Lisa was visiting because we laughed continuously. That was about the worst of it.

I try to follow my mom's actions when I'm angry about something because her way was always the right way. My sisters and I are very blessed to have had a wonderful mother and teacher."

*Joyce Pugliese O'Donnell, remembering her mother Mary Jane Cerchiaro Pugliese*

"My mother was a woman of few words, but her actions spoke volumes of the wonderful mother, wife, friend and neighbor she was.

She taught me the Golden Rule by showing me how to treat others with love and respect. She encouraged me to be myself, by allowing me to make my own mistakes but being available to help point out the important lessons learned. Her many examples of compassion and kindness toward others helped me become a faithful and loyal friend. Her unwavering faith in God showed me that every life situation can be faced as long as we place our complete trust in Him.

She taught me how to put on lipstick and blot my lips with a tissue, but more importantly that true beauty is found from within.

She taught me the joy of gardening and the careful tending of a rose bush.

She taught me the love of music by filling our house with it. She knew every word to all the Broadway musicals. She even named our pet canary "Perry" after Perry Como, the famous crooner of the fifties and sixties.

She taught me how to sew, sing, and soar using my God-given talents.

Not only did she give me life, she taught me how to live."

*Marcia Pugliese Russotto, remembering her mother Mary Jane Cerchiaro Pugliese*

# PART TWO

# THE RECIPES

"…and men ate the bread of angels…"
Psalm 78 v. 25

# ABOUT THE RECIPES

These recipes are not for food snobs or "foodies," as they endearingly refer to themselves. You won't find the words deglaze, reduce, or julienne. They do not reflect updated, contemporary tastes or trends. For example, the ingredient "oleo" can be substituted with margarine. I don't think many people would know what oleo is, but I left it in for effect, just as I have left in "electric mixer."

My intent is to inspire you to experience and enjoy these original recipes for their simple, basic, and unpretentious preparation. These recipes are very personal to me and are reminiscent of the Italian culture I grew up with. I hope they capture the simplicity and love with which they were prepared and served to family and friends.

Many of these recipes did not exist on paper. I crafted recipes after many preparations in the kitchen. For some, I relied on the memory of family and friends. My goal is to capture the spirit of the authentic Italian cook whose main objective is preparing the best possible meal with the freshest possible ingredients, pure and simple.

# CAKES FOR ALL OCCASIONS
## CASSATA

A s far back as I can remember, once a month my mother was on the schedule with the rest of the members of the Christian Mothers' Association to bake a cake for Sunday Night Bingo. These cakes were sliced and served by the piece for twenty-five cents; coffee was available for a dime. This monthly event gave the women of Sharpsburg a chance to show off their skill in the kitchen.

Another similar occasion was the annual church bake sale. This was really a fundraiser / competition. The cakes were sold by the slice and it was easy to tell whose cake was the best as it was the one that disappeared the fastest.

Theresa Sisco was Sharpsburg's most renowned baker. She baked a wedding cake for almost every couple that married in Sharpsburg. Her delicious cakes were to die for—or should I say to marry for? She baked one type of wedding cake: a traditional white almond-flavored batter with a creamy egg custard filling with fresh strawberries. Her filling is what made her cakes so exceptional. After Theresa assembled the cake with all its tiers, she covered it with a light and velvety whipped cream frosting. I can honestly say that I have never tasted a wedding cake better than Theresa's, and I have attended *many* weddings. I'm sorry to report that

Theresa's recipe is not available as she took it to her grave. But here is a sampling of other sweet and delicious confections made by the women of Sharpsburg.

## GOLDEN GLOW CAKE WITH CHOCOLATE FROSTING

| | |
|---|---|
| 2 cups | cake flour |
| 2 ½ teaspoons | baking powder |
| 1 teaspoon | salt |
| 1 ¼ cup | sugar |
| ¼ cup | shortening |
| ¼ cup | butter |
| ¾ cup | milk, divided |
| 2 | eggs |
| 1 teaspoon | vanilla |

Preheat oven to 350 degrees. Sift together the flour, baking powder, salt, and sugar. Add shortening, butter, and ½ cup milk. Beat for two minutes with electric mixer until batter is well blended and glossy. Add remaining ¼ cup milk, two eggs, and vanilla. Beat for two minutes. Pour batter into two greased and floured 8" cake pans. Bake for 30 to 35 minutes. Cool. Ice with chocolate butter frosting.

## CHOCOLATE BUTTER FROSTING

| | |
|---|---|
| ¼ cup | butter or oleo |
| 2 cups | sifted confectioner's sugar |
| 1 ½ | one ounce square unsweetened chocolate, melted |
| 2 | egg yolks |
| 1 teaspoon | vanilla |
| 1 tablespoon | cream or milk |

Thoroughly cream butter and half of the sugar, adding the melted chocolate after half the sugar is added. Add rest of sugar. Stir in the egg yolks and vanilla. Add cream after frosting becomes thick. Makes enough to frost top and side of two 8" layers.

## BANANA BUTTERMILK CAKE

| | |
|---|---|
| 2 | cups sugar |
| 2 | sticks oleo |
| 3 | eggs |
| 4 | cups flour |
| 1 ½ | teaspoon baking soda |
| ½ | teaspoon baking powder |
| ½ | teaspoon salt |
| 3 | bananas, mashed |
| ½ | cup buttermilk |

Preheat oven to 350 degrees. Cream sugar and oleo. Add eggs and mix till well blended. Sift dry ingredients together and add to creamed mixture. Add bananas and buttermilk, alternating. Bake one hour in a greased and floured tube pan. Cool, remove from pan, and dust with confectioner's sugar.

## STRAWBERRY CAKE

| 1 | white cake mix |
| 4 | egg whites, unbeaten |
| 1 | small package frozen strawberries |
| 1 | small package strawberry Jell-O |

Preheat oven to 350 degrees. Mix all ingredients in electric mixer for two minutes. Pour into a greased and floured 9"x 13" pan and bake for 30-35 minutes. Top with whipped cream and fresh strawberries.

## POUND CAKE

| ½ pound | butter |
| ½ pound | oleo |
| 1 box | powdered sugar (one pound) |
| 6 | whole eggs |
| 3 cups | flour |
| 1 teaspoon | vanilla |

Preheat oven to 350 degrees. Beat butter and oleo together. Gradually add powdered sugar and beat. Then add eggs one at a time, beating after each addition. Then beat for fifteen minutes. Gradually add flour and then vanilla. Grease tube pan and pour in batter. Bake one hour. This freezes well.

# SOUP FOR A SICK FRIEND
# ZUPPA

S oup is one of the most basic of recipes and is a staple in the Italian kitchen. I believe that you add love to a pot of simmering homemade soup with every stir and each added ingredient. What could be better than the wonderful aroma released each time you lift the soup lid?

The soups in this book often found their way to the home of a sick friend or a neighbor in need. Served with a salad and a loaf of warm Italian bread, these soups frequently became a meal on a busy day.

## CHICKEN PASTINA SOUP

| | |
|---|---|
| 1 | whole chicken, cut up |
| ½ cup | chopped onion |
| 2 | carrots, sliced |
| 2 | stalks celery, sliced |
| ½ lb. | Acini de Pepe (pastina pasta) |
| 1 large can | chicken broth |
| Salt and pepper to taste | |

Place chicken pieces in large stock pot and cover with cold water. Place lid on pot and simmer over low-med heat for 30-40 minutes. Periodically skim the foam from the top with a slotted spoon. Remove chicken pieces, let cool, remove meat from bones and cut in bite-size pieces, and return to stock pot with chopped vegetables, salt and pepper to taste, and can of chicken broth. Simmer on low until vegetables are soft—about 30 minutes. Add ½ box of pastina. Simmer for ten minutes till done. You can add tiny meatballs to the broth while the vegetables cook. Serve this soup with lots of parmesan cheese.

## MEATBALLS FOR SOUP

| | |
|---|---|
| 1 pound | ground chuck or combination beef, veal and pork |
| 2 | eggs, beaten |
| ¼ cup | parmesan cheese |
| ¼ cup | dry seasoned breadcrumbs |
| 2 | cloves garlic, through press |
| 1 tablespoon | flat leaf parsley |
| Salt and pepper to taste | |

Mix all ingredients in large bowl. Roll into small balls, ¾ to one inch diameter. Add to soup with vegetables.

## LENTIL SOUP

| | |
|---|---|
| 8 ounces | dry lentils |
| 2 tablespoons | olive oil |
| 2-3 | cloves garlic, minced |
| 1 | small onion, chopped |
| 1 | stalk celery, chopped |
| ¼ pound | pancetta or bacon, diced |
| 64 ounces | chicken broth |
| 1 | bay leaf |
| ½ cup | marinara sauce, bought or homemade |
| 1 cup | small pasta (shells, ditalini, pastina) |
| Salt and pepper to taste | |

Sort and rinse lentils, set aside. In large stock pot, heat oil. Add onion, celery, garlic, and pancetta. Cook till vegetables are tender and pancetta is crisp. Add lentils, chicken broth and bay leaf, season to taste. Bring to boil, reduce heat, cover and simmer 20 minutes or till lentils are tender. Add tomato sauce and pasta and cook for another 10 minutes. Add hot water if soup is too thick. Remove bay leaf and serve with a drizzle of olive oil and parmesan cheese.

Note—You can substitute the pasta with two small potatoes. Dice the potatoes and add them with the lentils.

## PASTA FAGIOLI
## (PASTA AND BEANS)

| | |
|---|---|
| 1 | small onion, chopped |
| 1 | stalk celery, chopped |
| 2 | cloves garlic, crushed or minced |
| 2 tablespoons | olive oil |
| 1 large can | crushed Italian tomatoes, (any brand you prefer, but we always use "6 in 1" brand) |
| 1 small can | tomato paste |
| 1 small can | water (use the paste can) |
| 2 cans | cannellini beans (you can use navy or cici or red beans, also) |
| 1 cup | small pasta (shells, ditalini, elbows) |

Fresh chopped parsley, parmesan cheese
Salt and pepper to taste

In large sauce pan, heat olive oil and add vegetables. Cook about 5 minutes. Add tomatoes, paste, and water. Cook 10 to 12 minutes. Add pasta and about another cup of water and cook till pasta is *al dente*, 7 to 8 minutes. Add beans, parsley, and cheese and cook a few more minutes. Serve with more cheese.

## MINESTRONE

| | |
|---|---|
| 2 | carrots, peeled and sliced |
| ½ pound | potatoes, peeled and diced |
| 2 | stalks celery, sliced |
| 2 | zucchini, diced |
| 2 | onions, chopped |
| 3 | cloves garlic, chopped |
| ¼ wedge | green cabbage, cut in thin strips |
| 6 tablespoons | olive oil, divided |
| 1 can | chopped tomatoes (15 ounces) |
| 3 tablespoons | tomato paste |
| Small bunch | chopped fresh basil leaves |
| 1 can | white beans, drained |
| ½ cup | small pasta (ditalini, elbows, etc.) |

Grated parmesan cheese
Salt and pepper to taste

In large stock pot, heat 4 tablespoons olive oil and add onions, carrots, celery, and one clove of garlic and cook till soft, about 5 minutes. Add tomatoes with juice, paste, 2 tablespoons chopped basil, two quarts water, salt and pepper to taste. Cover and simmer for 20 minutes, stirring occasionally. Add potatoes and zucchini, cover, cook 10 minutes. Add cabbage, cook 15 minutes more. Finally, add beans and pasta. Cook uncovered for 10 minutes. At end of cooking, add remaining olive oil and the basil and chopped garlic. Check seasoning, adjust to taste. Water can be added, although this soup is meant to be thick. Sprinkle with parmesan cheese and serve.

## PUG'S MINEST'

| | |
|---|---|
| 1 large bunch | fresh spinach or escarole |
| 2 quarts | chicken stock |
| 1 pound | sweet or hot Italian sausage, sliced |
| 1 large | onion, chopped |
| 1 | green pepper, chopped |
| 2 | whole cloves garlic |
| 1 large can | crushed tomatoes |
| 15 ounces | red kidney beans |
| ½ teaspoon | oregano |
| ½ teaspoon | red pepper flakes |

Salt and pepper to taste

Rinse and trim and cut off stems of spinach or escarole, cut in strips. Place in large stock pot with chicken broth and cook till wilted.

Meanwhile in skillet, brown sausage, onion, pepper, and garlic till cooked through and vegetables are soft. Add to the stock pot containing the escarole, along with the can of tomatoes, the beans and the seasoning. Cook for 20 to 25 minutes. Add water to thin. Serve with grated parmesan cheese.

## CAULIFLOWER AND SPAGHETTI SOUP

| | |
|---|---|
| 1 ½ cups | cauliflower cut in bite-size pieces |
| 2 tablespoons | olive oil |
| 2 | cloves garlic, chopped |
| 32 ounces | chicken broth |
| ½ cup | marinara sauce (homemade or bought) |
| 1/3 box | spaghetti, broken in one inch pieces |

Salt and pepper to taste

Brown garlic and cauliflower in large saucepan with olive oil till tender, 5 to 7 minutes. Add chicken broth, bring to a boil. Add pasta and salt and pepper. Simmer for 6 to 8 minutes. Stir in marinara sauce. Ladle into bowls, drizzle with olive oil and sprinkle with parmesan cheese.

# PASTA, PASTA, PASTA

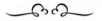

Pasta and tomato sauce hold an esteemed place of honor on every Italian table. Whether it's a holiday meal or a Sunday, there is always room for pasta. There are many different recipes for tomato sauce; many are very similar, varying only by an ingredient or spice. Each recipe evolved within a family according to that family's taste and the region from which the recipe originated in Italy. The availability of ingredients played a large part in the way the sauce is made. For some recipes, basil is the key flavor. Others rely on garlic or onion as the main flavor. Some people use crushed tomatoes while other prefer pureed. Pasta shapes vary across regions in Italy. Some areas use short tubular shapes, such as rigatoni or penne, while other regions prefer thin, long strands like spaghetti or linguine.

The following sauce recipe is my family's recipe. I learned how to make this sauce from my Nana, and my daughters have learned from me. I guarantee that if you make this sauce one time, you will never go down the jarred sauce aisle again!

## BASIC TOMATO SAUCE

| | |
|---|---|
| 3 tablespoons | olive oil |
| 2-3 | whole cloves garlic |
| 1 large can | crushed Italian tomatoes (we prefer "6 in 1" brand) |
| 8 ounces | tomato sauce |
| 1 small can | tomato paste |
| 1 teaspoon | dried oregano |
| 1-2 sprigs | fresh basil (basilacol) |
| Salt and pepper to taste | |

In a large stock pot over medium heat, sauté the garlic in the olive oil. Sauté till soft, but do not burn. Add crushed tomatoes, sauce, and paste and one or two cans of water (use the tomato paste can). Stir and cook for ten minutes. Add oregano, salt, pepper, and torn basil leaves. Reduce heat and simmer for 30 to 40 minutes. The basil gives the sauce its sweetness. If you like, and depending on what brand of tomatoes you use, you can add ½ teaspoon of sugar if you think the sauce is bitter. This makes enough sauce for one pound of pasta (with some left over).

Some Italian women simmer their sauce on low all day. This really isn't necessary, as it will be ready to serve over pasta in under an hour.

Note: Always use a wooden spoon when making sauce. This was enforced by Nana and my mother.

## BASIC MEATBALLS

| | |
|---|---|
| 1 ½ pounds | ground meat (the best is 1/3 beef, 1/3 pork and 1/3 veal) |
| 2 slices | torn, firm white bread (not soft packaged bread) |
| 2 or 3 tablespoons | milk |
| 2 | eggs, beaten |
| ½ cup | parmesan cheese |
| ½ cup | chopped onion |
| 3 tablespoons | chopped fresh parsley **or** 1 tablespoon dried parsley |
| 1 ½ teaspoons | salt |
| ¾ teaspoon | pepper |

Place meat in a large bowl, set aside. Tear the bread into small pieces, about the size of your fingernail, and put it in a medium mixing bowl. Pour milk over the bread and let it soak a few minutes. Add the beaten eggs, cheese, onion, parsley, and salt and pepper to the bread. Stir the ingredients till well mixed. Add this mixture to the ground meat and mix with your hands until everything holds together. Lightly shape the mixture into 2-inch balls. The more you handle the mixture, the tougher the meatball will be!

Heat about ¼ cup olive oil in a large skillet with minced garlic. Brown the meatballs on all sides. (They will finish cooking in the sauce.) Transfer meatballs to a paper towel-lined plate to drain some of the oil. Add the meatballs to a pot of basic tomato sauce and continue simmering for 30 minutes. Makes about 16 meatballs.

## MANICOTTI

| 6 | eggs |
|---|------|
| 3 cups | water |
| 3 cups | flour |
| 1 teaspoon | salt |

With whisk or electric mixer, mix ingredients until batter is free of lumps. The batter will be thin, like pancake mix. Grease a skillet only once with one tablespoon of oil. Drop two tablespoons of batter onto the skillet. If you want smaller manicotti, use less batter. Smooth the batter and form it into a circle with a spoon. When the pasta is shiny on top, it is done. Do not turn over. Place each finished manicotti on wax paper and continue with rest of batter.

## RICOTTA FILLING

| 24 ounces | ricotta cheese |
|-----------|----------------|
| ½ cup | parmesan cheese |
| 2 | eggs |
| 1 tablespoon | chopped flat leaf parsley |
| Salt and pepper to taste | |

Mix all ingredients until creamy. Fill each manicotti with one tablespoon of filling, roll up, and place side by side in 9 x 13 baking dish in a single layer. Cover with tomato sauce, parmesan cheese, and shredded mozzarella. Cover with foil and bake for 20 minutes. Remove foil and bake for 10 minutes in a 350 degree oven. Makes about two dozen manicotti.

## RAVIOLI

| | |
|---|---|
| 4 cups | flour |
| 3 | eggs |
| 1 tablespoon | water |
| 1 pound | ricotta cheese |
| 1 | egg |
| 2 tablespoons | parmesan cheese |
| ½ teaspoon | salt |
| 2 tablespoons | chopped flat leaf parsley |

Mix together flour, eggs, and water to make a dough and work until firm. Divide dough in two and roll into two thin sheets. Make cheese filling by combining remaining ingredients and mixing together thoroughly. Cut dough into two-inch squares and fill with one teaspoon of cheese mixture. Fold over so ends meet. Make sure edges are well closed after folding. This can be done by fluting the edges with a fork. Place ravioli on a clean dish towel and cover with another dish towel for 20 minutes. This lets the ravioli dry out a little. Cook ravioli in 5 quarts of salted, boiling water for 15 minutes or until they float to the top. You may have to do this in batches. Serve with tomato sauce. You can also bake the ravioli. Cover them with sauce and bake for about ½ hour at 350 degrees. This recipe easily serves 4-6 people.

Note: The traditional way to make the dough is as follows:

Place the flour on a large cutting board in a mound, making a "well" in the center. Add the beaten eggs and water and a pinch of salt in the center and mix gently with a fork, incorporating the flour into the egg mixture from the inside walls of the well. When the dough becomes too stiff to continue mixing with the fork, start kneading with your hands until you have a smooth, slightly sticky dough, about 10 minutes. Let rest for 10 minutes before you roll it out.

## PASTA AL FORNO
## (BAKED PASTA)

| 1 pound | pasta, any short tubular shape like penne, rigatoni, or mostaccioli |
| 4 cups | homemade or purchased tomato sauce with tiny meatballs |
| ½ cup | canned peas |
| 3 | hardboiled eggs, sliced |
| 1 cup | shredded mozzarella cheese |
| ½ cup | parmesan cheese |

Cook pasta *al dente*, drain and set aside. Layer a 9 x 13 baking dish as follows:

¼ cup sauce
½ of the cooked pasta
½ of sauce and meatballs
All of the peas
½ of both cheeses
All of the hardboiled eggs
Rest of pasta
Rest of sauce and meatballs
Rest of cheese

Cover with foil, bake in 350 degree oven for 25 minutes, taking foil off last 5 minutes.

## PASTINA AND RICOTTA

| ½ pound | pastina pasta |
| 15 ounces | ricotta cheese (whole milk or part skim) |
| 2 tablespoons | butter |
| Parmesan cheese | |

Bring salted water to a boil in large saucepan. Add the pastina. Cook, stirring frequently, until pasta is tender, about 8 minutes.

Scoop out ¼ cup of the cooking water and set aside. Drain pastina and place in a large bowl with the ricotta and butter. Mix well, adding the water if pasta seems dry. Sprinkle with parmesan cheese, season with salt and pepper to taste and serve immediately.

## SHELLS AND BROCCOLI

| One pound | medium size pasta shells |
| One head | broccoli cut in bite size pieces |
| 1/3 cup | olive oil |
| 2 cloves | minced garlic |
| ½ cup | parmesan cheese |
| Salt and pepper to taste | |

Bring salted water to a boil in a large stock pot. Add pasta to pot and cook; when pasta has about six minutes left, add broccoli. You also may cook the broccoli separately. Drain pasta and broccoli, saving some of the cooking water. Add minced garlic, oil and cheese to pasta. Add saved water to pasta if seems too dry. Season with salt and pepper and serve immediately. Pass red pepper flakes to anyone who wants an added kick to this dish.

# THE COOKIE TRAY

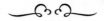

Italians love cookies. A holiday isn't a holiday and a wedding isn't a wedding without cookies. At my oldest daughter's wedding reception, we had the wait staff process out of the kitchen into the dining room carrying cookie trays over their heads. All of this while the band played the theme song from *The Godfather*. Very Corleone-ish!

## ALMOND BISCOTTI

| | |
|---|---|
| ¾ cup | whole almonds |
| 3 | eggs |
| 1 teaspoon | vanilla extract |
| ½ teaspoon | almond extract |
| 2 cups | all purpose flour |
| ¾ cup | sugar |
| 1 teaspoon | baking soda |
| Dash of salt | |

Place nuts in a shallow pan and bake in a 350 degree oven for 8 to 10 minutes, or until golden brown. Let cool. In a small bowl, beat eggs, vanilla, and almond extract with a wire whisk. In a mixing bowl, combine flour, sugar, baking soda, and salt. Add egg mixture and blend one minute. Cut nuts into halves or thirds and mix in. Divide dough in half. On a greased and floured baking sheet, pat out dough into two logs about ½ inch wide and 12 inches long. Space them at least 2 inches apart. Bake in the middle of a 300 degree oven for 45 minutes or until golden brown. Transfer from the baking sheet to rack. Let cool for 5 minutes. Place on large cutting board. With a serrated knife, slice diagonally at a 45-degree angle about ½-inch thick. Lay the slices flat on the baking sheet and return to a 275 degree oven for 20 to 25 minutes or until toasted, turning them over once to dry the other side. Makes 3 1/2 to 4 dozen.

Store in a tightly covered container.

## CHOCOLATE GLAZE VARIATION

Coarsely chop 3 ounces semisweet chocolate and place in a small pan that fits snugly over a saucepan of barely simmering water. Heat until chocolate melts. Stir to blend. With a spatula, spread over entire top of one side of cookie. Let cool at room temperature until set.

## SOUR CREAM COOKIES

| | |
|---|---|
| ½ cup | shortening or oleo |
| 1 ½ cups | sugar |
| 2 | eggs |
| 1 cup | sour cream |
| 2 ¾ cups | flour |
| ½ teaspoon | baking soda |
| ½ teaspoon | baking powder |
| ½ teaspoon | salt |
| 1 teaspoon | vanilla |

Preheat oven to 400 degrees. Cream shortening and sugar. Add beaten eggs. Sift dry ingredients; add alternately with sour cream. Add vanilla. Drop by teaspoonful on prepared cookie sheet. Bake for 10 minutes. Cool on rack and then frost with powdered sugar frosting (2-½ cups confectioner's sugar, 2 tablespoons melted butter, and 5 tablespoons water. Combine all ingredients and spread on cookie, decorate with sprinkles and jimmies.)

## PIZZELLES

| | |
|---|---|
| 6 | eggs |
| 1 cup | melted and cooled shortening |
| 1 ½ cups | sugar |
| Pinch of salt | |
| 1 tablespoon | anise seeds, **or** |
| 1 teaspoon | pure anise oil (found in drug stores) |
| 1 teaspoon | vanilla flavoring |
| 3 ½ cups | flour |

Beat eggs, add melted and cooled shortening. Beat and add sugar, salt, and flavorings. Beat until well mixed. Add flour gradually, mixing well. Usually, the last cup of flour has to be mixed with a spoon because the dough gets too heavy for mixer.

Put a teaspoon of dough in center of a well heated electric pizzelle iron. Close the lid, hold the handle down and count to 40. Lift the lid. The cookie should be light golden and lift off easily with a butter knife. Place on rack to cool. Repeat with remaining batter.

These keep in an airtight container for 2 or 3 weeks. Makes about 6 dozen.

## SNOWBALLS

| | |
|---|---|
| 1 cup | butter or margarine, softened |
| ½ cup | confectioner's sugar |
| 1 teaspoon | vanilla |
| 2 ¼ cups | flour |
| ¼ teaspoon | salt |
| ¾ cup | finely chopped walnuts |

Preheat oven to 400 degrees. Mix thoroughly the butter, sugar, and vanilla. Work in flour, salt, and nuts until dough holds together. Shape the dough into 1-inch balls and place on ungreased cookie sheet. Bake 10 to 12 minutes or until set but not brown. While warm, roll in confectioner's sugar. Cool. Makes about 4 dozen.

## ITALIAN KNOTS

| | |
|---|---|
| 3 | eggs |
| ¾ cup | sugar |
| ½ cup | milk |
| ½ cup | shortening, melted |
| 1 teaspoon | vanilla, or anise flavoring |
| 3 cups | flour |
| 3 teaspoons | baking powder |
| ½ teaspoon | salt |

Beat eggs well. Add sugar and milk gradually, continue beating. Add shortening, beat. Add flavoring, beat. Sift flour, baking powder, and salt together in separate bowl. Add flour mixture 1 cup at a time to liquid mixture. Dough will be soft and sticky. Wrap in waxed paper and refrigerate for 1 hour.

Preheat oven to 350 degrees and lightly grease two cookie sheets.

Place dough on well-floured surface. Pinch off about 1 tablespoon of dough and roll on surface with your hands and roll each piece into a 6 or 7 inch rope the width of your finger. Tie into a loose knot and place 1 inch apart on cookie sheet. Bake for 12 to 14 minutes until lightly brown. Cool slightly. Frost while warm.

## ITALIAN KNOT FROSTING

Combine 1-1/2 cups sifted confectioner's sugar, 4 table-spoons milk or water, and 1 teaspoon vanilla flavoring. Beat until smooth; add more liquid to make a thinner consistency. You can add food coloring if you'd like.

Dip the top of each cookie in frosting and shake off excess. Place on wax paper or rack and sprinkle with colored sprinkles. Let dry completely before storing. Will keep up to a week in airtight container or freeze for up to three months.

## SESAME COOKIES

| | |
|---|---|
| 3 ½ cups | flour |
| 1 tablespoon | baking powder |
| 2/3 cup | sugar |
| ½ cup | lard, or ¼ cup lard and ¼ cup margarine* |
| 2 | large eggs, beaten |
| | grated zest of one orange |
| 2 tablespoons | orange juice |
| 2/3 cup | milk |
| 1 | egg beaten with 1 tablespoon water |
| 2 cups | sesame seeds |

Preheat oven to 350 degrees. Lightly grease 2 cookie sheets. In a bowl, mix the flour and baking powder together, then add the sugar and mix. Add the lard (and margarine) and work it into the flour mixture until it resembles cornmeal. Add the eggs and orange zest, and orange juice. Then add the milk a little at a time and work the mixture until a ball of dough forms.

Divide the dough into 4 pieces. Roll each piece on a floured surface into a rope about 18 inches long and the thickness of your middle finger. Cut the ropes into 2-inch pieces. Beat the egg with the water to make a wash. Dip each piece into the egg wash and roll in the sesame seeds to coat on all sides. Place one inch apart on the cookie sheets. Bake for 20 to 25 minutes, or until nicely browned. Transfer to wire racks to cool.

*Lard gives the cookies the right texture and flavor.

# ASSORTIDA

A friend of mine was in a bakery. She overheard a worker ask an older Italian lady what she wanted to have. The woman answered "assortida." My friend and I took her answer to mean an assortment. I liked this word and so I've dedicated this last section to an "assortida" of breads, pizza, and holiday dishes.

I do wish you would try as many of my family recipes as you can. Growing up I took these wonderful dishes and dinners for granted. My goal now is to preserve them for future generations.

## NANA'S PIZZA BIANCA

### BASIC DOUGH

| | |
|---|---|
| 1 package | dry yeast (one envelope) |
| 1 ¾ cups | luke warm water |
| 1 teaspoon | salt |
| 4 ½ to 5 cups | flour |
| Olive oil | |

In a large bowl, dissolve the yeast in about ¼ cup of warm water. Allow to sit for five minutes. Add remaining water and salt. Add the flour one cup at a time—you might not need it all. Work the dough with your hands on a floured surface until it forms a ball. Knead dough for 5 or 10 minutes, turning dough over on itself until it is smooth, shiny and elastic.

Grease bowl with olive oil. Place dough in bowl, turning to coat with oil on all sides. Cover bowl with dish towel (as Nana did) or with plastic wrap. Keep in a draft free place (such as your oven, turned off) until it doubles in size. This should take about 1 hour.

When ready, punch the dough down on a floured surface and knead a few more times.

Divide dough in two, roll out each piece in a 12-inch circle and place on two well greased cookie or pizza trays.

## TOPPING

| 1/3 cup | olive oil |
| 1 cup | Italian, black cured olives, pits removed |
| 2 tablespoons | dried oregano |
| 1 cup | Grated romano or parmesan or both |

Divide olive oil, oregano, and cheese and top each pizza. Press the olives down into the dough. Bake in 400 degree oven for 15 or 20 minutes till bottom of pizza is golden brown. Slice and serve immediately.

## PITACHIDA

This is the Calabrese dialect for *pizza fritta*, or fried bread.

Make one recipe of Basic Dough. Once the dough has risen, tear off 12 pieces, about the size of an egg. Flatten each piece with your hand till it looks like an oval. Place on a dish towel for 20 to 30 minutes, until the dough rises a second time.

Heat oil in a deep fryer or a heavy pot to 375 degrees. You'll need at least 32 ounces.

Add three pieces of dough at a time and let fry for 3 or 4 minutes, until golden brown. Remove with a slotted spoon and place on paper towels or brown paper bags to drain. Sprinkle with sugar or salt. Serve hot.

## EASTER BREAD

| | |
|---|---|
| 1 ½ packages | yeast |
| ¼ cup | warm water |
| ½ pound | butter, melted |
| ½ quart | milk |
| 4 | eggs |
| 1 cup | sugar |
| 2 ½ pounds | flour |
| 1 tablespoon | anise seeds, optional |

Dissolve yeast in warm water, set aside. Melt butter and milk in saucepan over low heat. Remove from heat and set aside. When liquids have cooled, combine with dissolved yeast in a large mixing bowl. Combine sugar and flour and anise seeds in a bowl and set aside. Beat eggs and add to cooled milk and butter. Gradually add the flour mixture to the wet ingredients till incorporated. Mix till dough holds together in a ball. Dough will be sticky, but continue to knead on floured surface till smooth and elastic, adding flour as needed.

Place in oiled bowl and cover to rise for 45 to 50 minutes.

Place dough in greased loaf pan, covered for second rising, until doubled in size. Bake in 350 degree oven for 50 minutes or till golden. Cool for 10 minutes, take out of pan and rub butter on top of bread to give it a nice shine. Bread can be frozen when completely cooled.

## EASTER RICOTTA PIE

| | |
|---|---|
| 30 ounces | ricotta cheese |
| ½ cup | sugar |
| 1 tablespoon | flour |
| ½ teaspoon | salt |
| 1 teaspoon | vanilla extract |
| 1 teaspoon | grated orange peel |
| 4 | egg yolks |
| 1 tablespoon | white raisins |
| 1 tablespoon | diced candied citron |
| 2 tablespoons | slivered almonds or pine nuts, toasted |
| 1 | egg white, mixed with 1 tablespoon water |

Pie dough for 9 inch two-crusted pie; either homemade or bought

Lightly butter the bottom and sides of a 9 x 1 ½-inch springform or false-bottom tart pan. Place one rolled out circle of pie crust into the pan, gently pressing the pasty into the bottom and up the sides of pan. Pass a rolling pin over the rim of the pan, pressing down hard to trim off the excess pastry around the top.

Roll out remaining pie crust on lightly floured board into a rectangle about 12 inches long. With a pastry wheel or sharp knife, cut into long even strips about ½ inch wide.

Preheat oven to 350 degrees. Combine the ricotta cheese with ½ cup sugar, 1 tablespoon flour, ½ teaspoon salt, vanilla, grated orange peel, and egg yolks, and beat until they are thoroughly mixed. Stir in raisins and candied citron. Spoon filling into the pastry shell, spreading it evenly with a spatula. Sprinkle the top with slivered almonds or pine nuts, then weave or crisscross the pastry strips across the pie to make a lattice design. Brush the strips with the egg wash.

Bake on the middle shelf of the oven for 1 to 1 ¼ hour, or until crust is golden and filling is firm.

Cool pie on wire rack, slide off outer rim of pan, leaving bottom disk of pan in place. Or, if you prefer, loosen bottom crust with a wide metal spatula and slide the pie onto a round serving plate. Must be refrigerated.

## EASTER FRITTATA

| | |
|---|---|
| 12 | eggs |
| 8 ounces | sliced sopressata, or pepperoni |
| 2 cups | mozzarella cheese, *or* provolone and mozzarella, shredded |
| 1 cup | ricotta cheese |

Salt and pepper to taste

Beat eggs in mixing bowl, season with salt and pepper. In large skillet, brown slices of meat to render some of the fat, but don't make the meat too crisp. Slowly add all of the eggs and stir slowly as you would make scrambled eggs. Add the shredded cheese. When eggs are almost set, add the ricotta cheese in tablespoonfuls all over the eggs. Place lid on skillet, take off heat and let sit 10 minutes to finish cooking. Or you can put the skillet in the oven under the broiler for 5 minutes or until lightly browned on top. This allows you to serve the dish in pie shape slices. Pass the parmesan cheese and red pepper flakes.

## CHRISTMAS EVE SCALLOP SOUP

| | |
|---|---|
| 1 ½ pounds | scallops, washed, diced and drained |
| ¼ pound | pancetta |
| 6 tablespoons | butter |
| 2 cups | light cream |
| 1 stalk | celery, diced |
| 1 ½ cups | onion, chopped |
| 1 leek | sliced |
| 3 cups | clam juice |
| 3 cups | water |
| 1 ½ cups | sliced fresh mushrooms |
| ½ teaspoon | thyme |
| 6 sprigs | parsley, whole |
| 1 ½ pounds | potatoes, diced |
| 1 large can | tomatoes, diced |

Salt and pepper to taste

Dice pancetta, brown in large stock pot, and pour off fat. Add butter, onions, leeks, celery, mushrooms, and tomatoes. Cook over low heat for five minutes, covered. Add clam juice, water, thyme, parsley, and salt and pepper. Cook for 30 minutes. Add potatoes and cook 20 minutes. Add scallops, cook 10 minutes. Discard parsley, stir in cream. Add sherry, if desired.

Printed in the United States
119449LV00001B/106-111/P